Lecture Notes in Computer Science   13823

More information about this series at https://link.springer.com/bookseries/558

Jana Fragemann · Jianning Li · Xiao Liu ·
Sotirios A. Tsaftaris · Jan Egger ·
Jens Kleesiek (Eds.)

Medical Applications with Disentanglements

First MICCAI Workshop, MAD 2022
Held in Conjunction with MICCAI 2022
Singapore, September 22, 2022
Proceedings

Editors
Jana Fragemann
Essen University Hospital
Essen, Germany

Jianning Li
Graz University of Technology
Graz, Austria

Xiao Liu
University of Edinburgh
Edinburgh, UK

Sotirios A. Tsaftaris
University of Edinburgh
Edinburgh, UK

Jan Egger
Graz University of Technology
Graz, Austria

Jens Kleesiek
German Cancer Consortium
Essen, Germany

ISSN 0302-9743   ISSN 1611-3349 (electronic)
Lecture Notes in Computer Science
ISBN 978-3-031-25045-3   ISBN 978-3-031-25046-0 (eBook)
https://doi.org/10.1007/978-3-031-25046-0

This Springer imprint is published by the registered company Springer Nature Switzerland AG
The registered company address is: Gewerbestrasse 11, 6330 Cham, Switzerland

Preface

Machine Learning applications have become very successful in recent years. In particular, deep learning (DL) has received a lot of attention and been included in many challenges in the medical field, including tasks such as segmentation, classification, and image generation. However, DL lacks some of the most important features expected in medical application: trustworthiness and interpretability. Most neural networks operate like black boxes and do not offer a way to understand the decision process. Shortcut learning can lead to wrong predictions or bad generalization. Especially in health care, these are huge problems as patients' lives and well-being are affected. Thus, reliable, trustworthy and understandable methods are needed. Therefore, looking more closely into a neural network can help. Most models use a so-called latent space representation, a different representation of the information given in the data. Giving this latent space some interpretable and controllable structure helps overcome the black box characteristic and highlights the features a network learns to make decisions. Therefore, this workshop addressed the topic of *disentanglement*. This was the first time we held the *Medical Applications with Disentanglements* (MAD) workshop at the MICCAI conference.

Our review process was double blind and we had two to three reviewers per paper. We accepted eight papers. One of these papers is a short one (seven pages). All others have at least ten pages. Furthermore, we added an introductory paper to outline the beginning of the topic. The accepted papers cover generative adversarial networks (GAN), variational autoencoders (VAE) and normalizing-flow architectures as well as a wide range of medical applications, like brain age prediction, skull reconstruction and unsupervised pathology disentanglement. We thank Zhaodi Deng for the flyer design and Kelsey L. Pomykala for proofreading.

September 2022

Jana Fragemann
Jianning Li
Xiao Liu
Sotirios A. Tsaftaris
Jan Egger
Jens Kleesiek

Organization

Organizing Committee

Jana Fragemann   Institute for Artificial Intelligence in Medicine,
                              Germany
Jianning Li   Institute for Artificial Intelligence in Medicine,
                              Germany
Jan Egger   Institute for Artificial Intelligence in Medicine,
                              Germany
Jens Kleesiek   Institute for Artificial Intelligence in Medicine,
                              Germany
Sotirios A. Tsaftaris   University of Edinburgh, UK
Xiao Liu   University of Edinburgh, UK
Zhiming Cui   ShanghaiTech University, China
Vivek Sharma   Harvard University, USA

Program Committee

Alejandro F. Frangi   University of Leeds, UK
Anirban Mukhopadhyay   TU Darmstadt, Germany
Asja Fischer   Ruhr University Bochum, Germany
Constantin Seibold   Karlsruhe Institute of Technology, Germany
Daniel Rückert   Imperial College London, UK
Felix Nensa   Institute for Artificial Intelligence in Medicine,
                              Germany
Johannes Kraus   University of Duisburg-Essen, Germany
Jörg Schlötterer   Institute for Artificial Intelligence in Medicine,
                              Germany
Kai Ueltzhöffer   EMBL Heidelberg, Germany
Keyvan Farahani   National Cancer Institute, Rockville, MD, USA
Klaus H. Maier-Hein   German Cancer Research Center, Germany
Michael Kamp   Institute for Artificial Intelligence in Medicine,
                              Germany
Nicola Rieke   NVIDIA, Germany
Nishant Ravikumar   University of Leeds, UK
Robert Seifert   University Hospital Essen, Germany
Seppo Virtanen   University of Leeds, UK
Seyed-Ahmad Ahmadi   NVIDIA, Germany
Shadi Albarqouni   University Hospital Bonn, Germany

Victor Alves   University of Minho, Portugal

Additional Reviewers

Frederic Jonske   Institute for Artificial Intelligence in Medicine,
                                       Germany
Jiahong Ouyang   Stanford University, USA

Contents

Introduction

Applying Disentanglement in the Medical Domain: An Introduction for the MAD Workshop

Jana Fragemann[1(✉)], Xiao Liu[2], Jianning Li[1,3,4], Sotirios A. Tsaftaris[2,5], Jan Egger[1,3,4,6], and Jens Kleesiek[1,6,7]

[1] Institute for AI in Medicine (IKIM), University Hospital Essen (AöR), Girardetstraße 2, 45131 Essen, Germany
{jana.fragemann,jianning.li,jan.egger,jens.kleesiek}@uk-essen.de
[2] School of Engineering, The University of Edinburgh, Edinburgh EH9 3FG, UK
{xiao.liu,s.tsaftaris}@ed.ac.uk
[3] Institute of Computer Graphics and Vision (ICG), Graz University of Technology (TUG), Inffeldgasse 16, 8010 Graz, Austria
{jianning.li,egger}@icg.tugraz.at
[4] Computer Algorithms for Medicine Laboratory, Graz, Austria
[5] The Alan Turing Institute, London NW1 2DB, UK
[6] Cancer Research Center Cologne Essen (CCCE), University Hospital Essen (AöR), Hufelandstraße 55, 45147 Essen, Germany
[7] German Cancer Consortium (DKTK), Partner Site Essen, Hufelandstraße 55, 45147 Essen, Germany

Abstract. For medical applications, trustworthiness, interpretability, and robustness are necessary properties of (deep) neural networks. For generative models, one approach towards this could be analyzing and structuring the latent space representation. In this context, the term *disentanglement* is often used, but still not uniquely defined. In 2022, we organized the first workshop about Medical Applications with Disentanglements (MAD) at the MICCAI conference in Singapore (https://mad.ikim.nrw/). The workshop had a general call for disentanglement papers in the medical field and the submitted papers are published in a Springer challenge proceedings. The aim of the introduction paper of this proceeding is to present the necessary background information for them. Thus, we give a short overview of this field and how challenges for deep learning in healthcare could be addressed with the help of disentanglement.

Keywords: Disentanglement · Generative models · Deep learning · MAD Workshop · MICCAI

1 Introduction

One main finding of two recent meta-reviews in non-medical deep learning [10], and medical deep learning [9] was that trained deep learning models are still considered black boxes, which cannot be understood in detail, in contrast to classic engineering-like algorithms, where every step can, in general, be understood. This means failure cases can often be 'debugged', which is mostly not the case for training networks with millions of nodes and weights, etc. Especially in healthcare, this leads to problems when it comes to the certification of deep learning approaches. In contrast to single cases with single pathologies, where the deep learning result can still be (double) checked manually after it ran, multiple cases or scans, or a whole body analysis can be unfeasible in clinical routine or even a reasonable offline time. One solution is to 'freeze' a training model, and reinforcement or even retraining needs, in general, a new certification (and freezing) process. This, however, seems only to provide a first or intermediate solution, optimally trained models can be better understood (even when the understanding is only in an automated way) in more detail.

Paying attention to the internal representation of deep learning models, the latent space, may offer some clues and possibilities to overcome their black box characteristics and increase trustworthiness and interpretability. Giving this hidden representation an interpretable structure can be seen as *disentanglement*. Bengio et al. [1] already mentioned the term *Disentangling Factors of Variation* in 2013 as a possible robust approach for feature learning.

In 2022, we organized the first workshop about Medical Applications with Disentanglements (MAD) at the MICCAI conference in Singapore. The workshop had a general call for disentanglement papers in the medical field:

– Disentanglement Definitions
– Disentanglement Metrics
– Analyzing Existing Models or Metrics
– Application of Disentanglement Methods onto - Medical/Clinical Datasets
– New Disentanglement Models
– Mathematical Background/Theory

The submitted and reviewed papers are published in a Springer challenge proceedings. And the aim of the introduction paper of this proceeding, is to present the necessary background information for them.

The rest of this paper is organized as follows. In Sect. 2, we introduce generative models and highlight visualization techniques that help to give an inside view of the decision process of neural networks. In Sect. 3, we discuss the term disentanglement and propose some definitions. In the next Sect. 4, we outline the challenges for medical applications in the context of disentanglement and give a short inside look into data set biases, availability and other aspects. The subsequent Sect. 5, list briefly some medical applications using disentanglement. The following Sect. 6, gives future directions with a focus on causality and disentanglement and evaluating disentanglement. The final Sect. 7 concludes this introduction paper.

2 Generative Models

In general, Deep Learning networks can be divided into two categories: *discriminative* and *generative* models. Some of the most popular generative models are Variational Autoencoders (VAEs) [20], Generative Adversarial Networks (GANs) [14] and Flow-based models [7]. Recently, Diffusion models [6] and transformer-based models [8] have become more and more popular. All of these models have been applied to medical data [12,15,38–40]. But in general, the black box characteristic remains. Different methods exist to understand the decision process of a network. Visualization techniques help to give an inside view into the decision process of neural networks, for example:

1. Saliency Maps [35]: For the saliency map every pixel of an input image is ranked by its importance with a score that is computed for one class.
2. Deep Visualisation [41]: In [41], two visualization techniques are introduced. One to show the activations that occured on every layer of a network and another one using regularized optimization in the input space to show learned features at every layer.
3. Grad Cam [3]: The Gradient-weight Class Activation Mapping is a technique to highlight the aspect of an input image that influences the prediction process by visualizing the gradient of the input sliding into the last convolutional layer. Up to the authors, this helps to detect possible failure concepts of a neural network or helps to reveal data set biases.

These techniques concentrated on convolutional classifiers, but can also be applied to other convolutional networks, e.g., [2].

Considering their latent space representation and giving it some structure and interpretability may also be a way out of the black box. Several developments of this *disentanglement* exists, e.g [5] or [17], applying different approaches with respect to the network architecture.

For generative models with a latent space representation, another way to analyze the decision process can be an interpretable structure of the latent space features. Assuming that an image results from a generating process based on simple features. Like for Dall-e [32], you just give some buzzwords, and the models generate an image. *Real* generative factors need to be more detailed, e.g., even for simple images like the ones from dSprites [26] a lot of factors, e.g., a simple white square on black background still needs *position, size, rotation*. At the same time, biases like shape, background color, object color, and image size are needed to be given as biases. If the latent space of a model captures these features in a structured way, this can be denoted as *disentanglement*, see Sect. 3.1. The degree of this can be visualized with the *interventional robustness score* [36]. This score offers a way to measure the effect of changes in the generative factors or disruptive factors on the latent space representation without being architecture-dependent.

3   Disentanglement

The term *disentanglement* has no unique definition (so far). Often it is referred to as a change in a latent factor that results in a specific change in the output [1], see Fig. 1. For more detailed overviews and reviews, see [22] and [13].

3.1   Definitions of Disentanglement

To give insight into the different points of view of disentanglement, we list a few different definitions:

1. Higgins et al. [16] present a definition of disentanglement based on group and representation theory. They concentrate on data transformations, respectively, symmetry transformations.
2. Suter et al. [36] have a causality point of view on disentanglement. Disentanglement is characteristic of the causal data-generating process.
3. The authors of [19] defined a representation of an input x as disentangled if this representation results form a combination of a pointwise nonlinearity and a permutation of the ground truth latent variables.

3.2   The Different Types of Biases

According to Locattello et al. [24], it is not possible to guarantee that a generative model learns a disentangled representation without supervision or biases. Thus, it cannot be guaranteed that a disentangled representation will be found. Therefore, some constraints can be applied to encourage a disentangled representation. Different possible biases are:

1. Independence or Total Correlation:
   Like in beta-VAE [18] or TCVAE [4], the bias is to encourage independence between the distributions of the dimensions to result in a representation where the variables do not influence each other.

2. A priori knowledge:

   (a) Data knowledge:
       E.g. for the MNIST data set, http://yann.lecun.com/exdb/mnist/, a priori knowledge is sometimes used like the number of the latent space dimensions or to choose them as categorical, or continuous [5,23]. Another example is the content and style disentanglement for magnetic resonance (MR) images; see, e.g., [29].
   (b) Supervision:
       Especially if one factor of interest should be disentangled, a label for this factor helps to separate the information in the latent space, e.g., in [43].

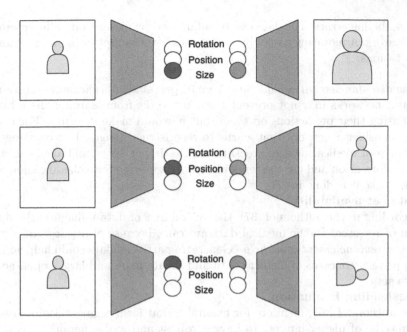

Fig. 1. The figure illustrates the idea of a disentangled representation in an example of an AutoEncoder (AE). Changing a value of the encoding (here illustrated through the color shift from red to orange) should lead to an specific change in the output. (Color figure online)

4 Challenges for Medical Applications

The authors Varoquaux and Cheplygina [37] give an excellent overview of recent challenges in the application of Deep Learning methods in healthcare. We pick up the following aspects of their analysis:

1. **Data set bias**:
   One of the core problems for the application of Deep Learning in medicine is the relatively small amount of data. Computer Vision applications often have access to data sets containing millions of images, like ImageNet (https://www.image-net.org/), while medical data sets usually only consist of thousands of scans from individuals [37]. But the authors of [37] strongly point out that bigger data sets are not the solution to every Deep Learning application in healthcare. They claim that often there is a problem with data set biases, like, e.g.:
   (a) *Spectrum bias* [30,37]: The collected patient data is not an adequate representation for all disease properties and patient conditions.
   (b) Shortcut learning: The authors of [37] mention an example of X-rays of patients with pneumothorax. A lot of these patients have a chest tube for treatment. The chest tube is not the reason for the pneumothorax. In [28], the authors also describe how *artifacts* or biases like this can influence the decision process of neural networks.

(c) Labeling errors: The data can be influenced by biases from different annotators. Annotating a scan by different experts can result in different annotations.

How disentanglement could help - An interpretable internal representation of neural networks may not prevent these networks from learning these biases or basing their predictions on them, but it would make it visible. For example., consider a network that learns to reconstruct images. If it captures the features of medical devices trackable in the latent space, one could exclude this information and use the remaining representation for a classification approach, like it is done in [27].

2. **Data set availability**:
   According to the authors of [37], the availability of data influences the direction of research. Public medical data are rare, because of privacy concerns.
   How disentanglement could help - Generating artificial data could help address the privacy concerns of medical data and create more and larger open-access data sets.

3. **Missleading Evaluation**:
   The authors of [37], mention, for example, that for a segmentation network, it may be of higher interest to have a robust and well-generalizing network that properly segments every pixel at the boundaries of a tumor.
   How disentanglement could help - Disentanglement cannot help concerning the evaluation context. But for generalization, it may be helpful, even if the results of the analysis until now are in general sobering [25].

5   Medical Applications

There are already numerous approaches using different ways of disentangled representations for medical applications. The applications range from brain age prediction with MR scans [11] to artifact reduction in CT scans [21] to the generation of molecules for drug discovery [31]. For more detailed reviews see [13] and [22].

6   Future Directions

6.1   Causality and Disentanglement

Schölkopf et al. [33], as well as Suter et al. [36] describe the connection between disentanglement and causality. Causality is a concept based on physical systems [33] and may help to overcome the generalization challenges of Deep Learning-based models. Schölkopf et al. [33] describe the difference between *statistical learning* and *causal learning*. Statistical learning can make predictions in independent and identical distributed (i.i.d.) settings, but cannot be reliably applied to distribution shifts, while causality-based models make predictions under interventions [33]. They describe disentanglement achieved through independent factors of variations as a special case of a trivial causal graph.

6.2   Evaluating Disentanglement

Several metrics exist [42] to measure the degree of disentanglement. But most of them measure different characteristics or properties, coming along with the different definitions of the term disentanglement. Furthermore, most of them need known ground truth factors leading to problems in real-world scenarios. Another problem is that some of these metrics contain some failure modes [34]. Thus, evaluation should be handled carefully. Therefore, future research aspects should include the development of a unique mathematical definition and more robust and unsupervised metrics.

7   Conclusion

In theory, getting a disentangled representation of a generative model seems to be promising and has a lot of advantages, especially in healthcare applications, where trustworthiness and reliability are needed. A lot of progress and applications have been made in practice, but there are still remaining pitfalls, making further research and experiments necessary.

Acknowledgments. This work received funding from 'KITE' (Plattform für KI-Translation Essen) from the REACT-EU initiative (https://kite.ikim.nrw/). Furthermore, We want to thank our workshop sponsors NVIDIA and HUAWEI.

The official *Medical Applications with Disentanglements (MAD)* workshop website for 2022 can be accessed under the following url: https://mad.ikim.nrw/.

References

1. Bengio, Y., Courville, A., Vincent, P.: Representation learning: a review and new perspectives. IEEE Trans. Pattern Anal. Mach. Intell. **35**(8), 1798–1828 (2013)
2. Brocki, L., Chung, N.C.: Concept saliency maps to visualize relevant features in deep generative models. In: 2019 18th IEEE International Conference on Machine Learning And Applications (ICMLA), pp. 1771–1778. IEEE (2019)
3. Chattopadhay, A., Sarkar, A., Howlader, P., Balasubramanian, V.N.: Grad-CAM++: generalized gradient-based visual explanations for deep convolutional networks. In: 2018 IEEE Winter Conference on Applications of Computer Vision (WACV), pp. 839–847. IEEE (2018)
4. Chen, R.T., Li, X., Grosse, R.B., Duvenaud, D.K.: Isolating sources of disentanglement in variational autoencoders. In: Advances in Neural Information Processing Systems, vol. 31 (2018)
5. Chen, X., Duan, Y., Houthooft, R., Schulman, J., Sutskever, I., Abbeel, P.: Info-GAN: interpretable representation learning by information maximizing generative adversarial nets. In: Advances in Neural Information Processing Systems, vol. 29 (2016)
6. Dhariwal, P., Nichol, A.: Diffusion models beat GANs on image synthesis. Adv. Neural. Inf. Process. Syst. **34**, 8780–8794 (2021)
7. Dinh, L., Krueger, D., Bengio, Y.: Nice: non-linear independent components estimation. arXiv:1410.8516 (2015)

8. Dosovitskiy, A., et al.: An image is worth 16x16 words: transformers for image recognition at scale. arXiv preprint arXiv:2010.11929 (2020)
9. Egger, J., et al.: Medical deep learning-a systematic meta-review. Comput. Methods Programs Biomed. 106874 (2022)
10. Egger, J., Pepe, A., Gsaxner, C., Jin, Y., Li, J., Kern, R.: Deep learning-a first meta-survey of selected reviews across scientific disciplines, their commonalities, challenges and research impact. PeerJ Comput. Sci. **7**, e773 (2021)
11. Fei, Y., Zhan, B., Hong, M., Wu, X., Zhou, J., Wang, Y.: Deep learning-based multimodal computing with feature disentanglement for MRI image synthesis. Med. Phys. **48**(7), 3778–3789 (2021). https://doi.org/10.1002/mp.14929. Epub 2021 Jun 7. PMID: 33959965
12. Ferreira, A., Li, J., Pomykala, K.L., Kleesiek, J., Alves, V., Egger, J.: GAN-based generation of realistic 3D data: a systematic review and taxonomy. arXiv preprint arXiv:2207.01390 (2022)
13. Fragemann, J., Ardizzone, L., Egger, J., Kleesiek, J.: Review of disentanglement approaches for medical applications - towards solving the gordian knot of generative models in healthcare (2022). https://doi.org/10.48550/ARXIV.2203.11132. https://arxiv.org/abs/2203.11132
14. Goodfellow, I.J., et al.: Generative adversarial networks. arxiv e-prints. arXiv preprint arXiv:1406.2661 (2014)
15. Heiliger, L., et al.: AutoPET challenge: combining nn-UNet with swin UNETR augmented by maximum intensity projection classifier (2022). https://doi.org/10.48550/ARXIV.2209.01112. https://arxiv.org/abs/2209.01112
16. Higgins, I., et al.: Towards a definition of disentangled representations. arXiv preprint arXiv:1812.02230 (2018)
17. Higgins, I., et al.: Beta-VAE: learning basic visual concepts with a constrained variational framework (2016)
18. Higgins, I., et al.: beta-VAE: learning basic visual concepts with a constrained variational framework. In: International Conference on Learning Representations (2017). https://openreview.net/forum?id=Sy2fzU9gl
19. Horan, D., Richardson, E., Weiss, Y.: When is unsupervised disentanglement possible? Adv. Neural. Inf. Process. Syst. **34**, 5150–5161 (2021)
20. Kingma, D.P., Welling, M.: Auto-encoding variational bayes. arXiv preprint arXiv:1312.6114 (2013)
21. Lee, J., Gu, J., Ye, J.C.: Unsupervised CT metal artifact learning using attention-guided beta-cycleGAN. IEEE Trans. Med. Imaging **40**(12), 3932–3944 (2021). https://doi.org/10.1109/TMI.2021.3101363
22. Liu, X., Sanchez, P., Thermos, S., O'Neil, A.Q., Tsaftaris, S.A.: Learning disentangled representations in the imaging domain. Med. Image Anal. **80**, 102516 (2022). https://doi.org/10.1016/j.media.2022.102516
23. Liu, X., Thermos, S., Sanchez, P., O'Neil, A.Q., Tsaftaris, S.A.: HSIC-InfoGAN: learning unsupervised disentangled representations by maximising approximated mutual information (2022). https://doi.org/10.48550/ARXIV.2208.03563. https://arxiv.org/abs/2208.03563
24. Locatello, F., et al.: Challenging common assumptions in the unsupervised learning of disentangled representations. In: Chaudhuri, K., Salakhutdinov, R. (eds.) Proceedings of the 36th International Conference on Machine Learning. Proceedings of Machine Learning Research, vol. 97, pp. 4114–4124. PMLR (2019). https://proceedings.mlr.press/v97/locatello19a.html
25. Locatello, F., et al.: A sober look at the unsupervised learning of disentangled representations and their evaluation. arXiv preprint arXiv:2010.14766 (2020)

26. Matthey, L., Higgins, I., Hassabis, D., Lerchner, A.: dSprites: disentanglement testing sprites dataset (2017). https://github.com/deepmind/dsprites-dataset/
27. Meng, Q., et al.: Mutual information-based disentangled neural networks for classifying unseen categories in different domains: application to fetal ultrasound imaging. IEEE Trans. Med. Imaging **40**(2), 722–734 (2020)
28. Nauta, M., Walsh, R., Dubowski, A., Seifert, C.: Uncovering and correcting shortcut learning in machine learning models for skin cancer diagnosis. Diagnostics **12**(1) (2022). https://doi.org/10.3390/diagnostics12010040. https://www.mdpi.com/2075-4418/12/1/40
29. Ouyang, J., Adeli, E., Pohl, K.M., Zhao, Q., Zaharchuk, G.: Representation disentanglement for multi-modal brain MRI analysis. In: Feragen, A., Sommer, S., Schnabel, J., Nielsen, M. (eds.) IPMI 2021. LNCS, vol. 12729, pp. 321–333. Springer, Cham (2021). https://doi.org/10.1007/978-3-030-78191-0_25
30. Park, S.H., Han, K.: Methodologic guide for evaluating clinical performance and effect of artificial intelligence technology for medical diagnosis and prediction. Radiology **286**(3), 800–809 (2018)
31. Polykovskiy, D., et al.: Entangled conditional adversarial autoencoder for de novo drug discovery. Mol. Pharm. **15**(10), 4398–4405 (2018). https://doi.org/10.1021/acs.molpharmaceut.8b00839. Epub 2018 Sep 19. PMID: 30180591
32. Ramesh, A., et al.: Zero-shot text-to-image generation (2021). https://doi.org/10.48550/ARXIV.2102.12092. https://arxiv.org/abs/2102.12092
33. Schölkopf, B., et al.: Toward causal representation learning. Proc. IEEE **109**(5), 612–634 (2021)
34. Sepliarskaia, A., Kiseleva, J., de Rijke, M.: How to not measure disentanglement. arXiv preprint arXiv:1910.05587 (2019)
35. Simonyan, K., Vedaldi, A., Zisserman, A.: Deep inside convolutional networks: visualising image classification models and saliency maps. arXiv preprint arXiv:1312.6034 (2013)
36. Suter, R., Miladinovic, D., Schölkopf, B., Bauer, S.: Robustly disentangled causal mechanisms: validating deep representations for interventional robustness. In: International Conference on Machine Learning, pp. 6056–6065. PMLR (2019)
37. Varoquaux, G., Cheplygina, V.: Machine learning for medical imaging: methodological failures and recommendations for the future. NPJ Digit. Med. **5**, 48 (2022). https://doi.org/10.1038/s41746-022-00592-y
38. Wei, R., Mahmood, A.: Recent advances in variational autoencoders with representation learning for biomedical informatics: a survey. IEEE Access **9**, 4939–4956 (2020)
39. Wilms, M., et al.: Invertible modeling of bidirectional relationships in neuroimaging with normalizing flows: application to brain aging. IEEE Trans. Med. Imaging **41**(9), 2331–2347 (2022)
40. Wolleb, J., Bieder, F., Sandkühler, R., Cattin, P.C.: Diffusion models for medical anomaly detection (2022). https://doi.org/10.48550/ARXIV.2203.04306. https://arxiv.org/abs/2203.04306
41. Yosinski, J., Clune, J., Nguyen, A., Fuchs, T., Lipson, H.: Understanding neural networks through deep visualization. arXiv preprint arXiv:1506.06579 (2015)
42. Zaidi, J., Boilard, J., Gagnon, G., Carbonneau, M.A.: Measuring disentanglement: a review of metrics. arXiv preprint arXiv:2012.09276 (2020)
43. Zhao, Q., Adeli, E., Honnorat, N., Leng, T., Pohl, K.M.: Variational AutoEncoder for regression: application to brain aging analysis. In: Shen, D., et al. (eds.) MICCAI 2019. LNCS, vol. 11765, pp. 823–831. Springer, Cham (2019). https://doi.org/10.1007/978-3-030-32245-8_91

GAN-Based Approaches

HSIC-InfoGAN: Learning Unsupervised Disentangled Representations by Maximising Approximated Mutual Information

Xiao Liu[1,4]($\boxtimes$), Spyridon Thermos[2], Pedro Sanchez[1,4], Alison Q. O'Neil[1,4], and Sotirios A. Tsaftaris[1,3,4]

[1] School of Engineering, University of Edinburgh, Edinburgh EH9 3FB, UK
Xiao.Liu@ed.ac.uk
[2] AC Codewheel Ltd., Edinburgh, UK
[3] The Alan Turing Institute, London, UK
[4] Canon Medical Research Europe Ltd., Edinburgh, UK

Abstract. Learning disentangled representations requires either supervision or the introduction of specific model designs and learning constraints as biases. InfoGAN is a popular disentanglement framework that learns unsupervised disentangled representations by maximising the mutual information between latent representations and their corresponding generated images. Maximisation of mutual information is achieved by introducing an auxiliary network and training with a latent regression loss. In this short exploratory paper, we study the use of the Hilbert-Schmidt Independence Criterion (HSIC) to approximate mutual information between latent representation and image, termed HSIC-InfoGAN. Directly optimising the HSIC loss avoids the need for an additional auxiliary network. We qualitatively compare the level of disentanglement in each model, suggest a strategy to tune the hyperparameters of HSIC-InfoGAN, and discuss the potential of HSIC-InfoGAN for medical applications.

Keywords: Disentangled representation learning · HSIC · InfoGAN

1 Introduction

Recently, machine learning (ML) and deep learning (DL) have achieved significant success in many computer science areas, for instance vision and natural language processing [12]. However, traditional fully supervised approaches cannot always be applied in specific domains such as medical imaging analysis, as the available annotations are limited due to the labeling process being tedious and costly. Thus, significant effort has been placed on alternative training methods such as unsupervised and semi-supervised learning. In particular, recent works [4,11,15] show that the typical unsupervised approach of disentangled representation learning without labeled data significantly boosts the performance of ML/DL models.

© The Author(s), under exclusive license to Springer Nature Switzerland AG 2023
J. Fragemann et al. (Eds.): MAD 2022, LNCS 13823, pp. 15–21, 2023.
https://doi.org/10.1007/978-3-031-25046-0_2

The widely agreed definition of a disentangled representation is one in which *"single latent units are sensitive to changes in single generative factors, while being relatively invariant to changes in other factors"* [2]. This definition is based on an implicit assumption that there is a generation process in the real world that translates independent generative factors to images. Hence, the overall goal in disentangled representation learning is to discover this generation process and the constituent generative factors from images. However, a comprehensive study [18] recently showed that it is impossible to learn a disentangled representation in an unsupervised setting, and all previous methods use various inductive biases or assumptions on either model design or learning process. Then, model performance largely depends on the introduced inductive biases that are tailored for specific tasks. In other words, different tasks require domain-specific expert knowledge to devise suitable inductive biases and assumptions.

As an unsupervised disentanglement method, InfoGAN [5] considers that the latent representations consist of categorical (we assume that we know the number of classes) and continuous latents. With this inductive bias, InfoGAN solves the information-regularised minimax game by jointly training a generator, a discriminator and an auxiliary network. In particular, the auxiliary network takes the generated image as input and is trained to correctly predict the corresponding latent representations of this image i.e. latent regression [26]. This forces the generated image to be highly dependent on the latent representations i.e. maximising the mutual information. Despite the cost of introducing an additional network/module, this strategy has been used in many disentanglement models such as [9,20,26].

In this paper, we examine the question of whether we can approximate mutual information between the latent representations and the generated image without the need for such an auxiliary network. We consider the Hilbert-Schmidt Independence Criterion (HSIC) [19] to approximate the mutual information between the latent representations and the generated image, termed HSIC-InfoGAN. HSIC is a kernel-based independence measurement. By projecting the inputs into kernel space, HSIC allows inputs to have different dimensionality. Directly optimising the HSIC loss removes the need for an auxiliary network, which could reduce the model training time and the memory load for saving model weights. As shown in our experiments, achieves satisfactory levels of disentanglement compared to InfoGAN. We further discuss a strategy to effectively tune the hyperparameters of HSIC-InfoGAN, and discuss its potential impact on medical applications.

2   Methodology

2.1   InfoGAN

Generative adversarial networks [8] train the generator G and discriminator D using a minimax game by optimising the following objective:

$$\min_{G} \max_{D} V(D, G) = \mathbb{E}_{\mathbf{X}}[\log D(\mathbf{X})] + \mathbb{E}_{\mathbf{z}}[\log(1 - D(G(\mathbf{z})))], \tag{1}$$

where $\mathbf{X}$ denotes an image sample and $\mathbf{z}$ is the noise vector. InfoGAN [5] proposes that the latent space contains the noise $\mathbf{z}$ as well as the disentangled latent code $\mathbf{c}$. To learn the disentangled representations, InfoGAN solves the information-regularised minimax game:

$$\min_{G} \max_{D} V_I(D, G) = V(D, G) - \lambda_I I(\mathbf{c}; G(\mathbf{z}, \mathbf{c})), \qquad (2)$$

where $I(\mathbf{c}; G(\mathbf{z}, \mathbf{c}))$ denotes the mutual information between the latent code $\mathbf{c}$ and the generated image $G(\mathbf{z}, \mathbf{c})$. However, we can only compute the exact and tractable mutual information for discrete variables or for specific problems that we know the probability distributions [1]. Due to the difficulty of directly max-imising the mutual information term, InfoGAN introduces an auxiliary network Q to derive the lower bound of the mutual information:

$$I(\mathbf{c}; G(\mathbf{z}, \mathbf{c})) \geq L_I(G, Q) = \mathbb{E}_{\mathbf{X}}[\mathbb{E}_{\mathbf{c}'}[\log Q(\mathbf{c}'|\mathbf{X})]]. \qquad (3)$$

Overall, the objective of InfoGAN is defined as:

$$\min_{G, Q} \max_{D} V_{\text{InfoGAN}}(D, G, Q) = V(D, G) - \lambda_{\text{InfoGAN}} L_I(G, Q). \qquad (4)$$

Note that most of the network weights of Q and D can be shared. Separate final (head) layers are used for the Q and D networks in InfoGAN.

2.2 Hilbert-Schmidt Independence Criterion (HSIC)

Considering the kernel function $k : \mathbb{R}^O \times \mathbb{R}^O \to \mathbb{R}$ where O denotes the image dimension, the HSIC loss is defined in [19] as:

$$\text{HSIC}(\mathbf{X}, \mathbf{z}) = (m - 1)^{-2} \text{trace}(K_{\mathbf{X}} H K_{\mathbf{z}} H), \qquad (5)$$

where $m \neq 1$ is the batch size in our case. $K_{\mathbf{X}_{ij}} = k(\mathbf{X}_i, \mathbf{X}_j)$ and $K_{\mathbf{z}_{ij}} = k(\mathbf{z}_i, \mathbf{z}_j)$ are the entries of $K_{\mathbf{X}} \in \mathbb{R}^{m \times m}$ and $K_{\mathbf{z}} \in \mathbb{R}^{m \times m}$. H is the centering matrix $H = I_m - \frac{1}{m} \mathbb{1}_m \mathbb{1}_m^T$. Following [19], we choose the Gaussian kernel $k(\mathbf{X}_i, \mathbf{X}_j) \sim exp(-\frac{1}{2}||\mathbf{X}_i - \mathbf{X}_j||^2/\sigma^2)$, where σ is a hyperparameter. Here, HSIC values are always positive and lower HSIC means higher independence (i.e. lower mutual information). Note that in Eq. 5, $\mathbf{X}$ and $\mathbf{z}$ can have different dimensionality i.e. they can be a tensor and a vector. We refer the readers to the section "Relating HSIC to Entropy" in [19] for a informal discussion about the relationship between HSIC and mutual information. Overall, mutual information is defined in terms of entropy that is related to volume [6], which can be considered as the product of the eigenvalues of the covariance matrix. HSIC is related to Frobenius norm that is a sum of the eigenvalues.

2.3 HSIC-InfoGAN

As discussed in [19], the mutual information can be approximated with HSIC. We propose to replace the mutual information term in InfoGAN with HSIC as an alternative. Using the HSIC loss we drop the need for an auxiliary network. It could potentially contribute to the stabilisation of InfoGAN training as there is no need for sharing the network weights of discriminator with the auxiliary network. Overall, HSIC-InfoGAN can be represented as:

$$\min_G \max_D V_{\text{HSIC}}(D, G) =$$
$$\mathbb{E}_{\mathbf{X}}[\log D(\mathbf{X})] + \mathbb{E}_{\mathbf{z},\mathbf{c}}[\log(1 - D(G(\mathbf{z}, \mathbf{c})))] - \lambda \text{HSIC}(\mathbf{X}, \mathbf{c}), \tag{6}$$

where λ is the weight of the HSIC loss. For HSIC-InfoGAN, the tunable hyperparameters are the kernel variance σ and loss weight λ. We will discuss the strategy to tune the two hyperparameters in detail in Sect. 3.

3   Experiments

3.1   Implementation Details

We perform experiments using the MNIST dataset [13] that contains 60,000 images of 10 digits with image size 28×28. All models are trained using the Adam optimiser [10] with a learning rate of $2 \times e^{-4}$ for the discriminator and $1 \times e^{-3}$ for the generator. Batch size is 100. We train the models for 100 epochs. Following [5], we set the dimension of $\mathbf{z}$ to 62 and the dimension of $\mathbf{c}$ to 12, where 10 dimensions of $\mathbf{c}$ represent categorical information (a 10-dimensional one-hot vector) and 2 dimensions of $\mathbf{c}$ represent continuous information (sampled from a uniform distribution $U(0, 1)$). All models are implemented in PyTorch [22] and are trained using an NVIDIA 2080 Ti GPU. The code for calculating the HSIC loss can be found in https://github.com/choasma/HSIC-Bottleneck.

3.2   Results

In Fig. 1, we share qualitative results for InfoGAN and HSIC-InfoGAN. c_1 and c_2 are the two continuous latent codes. For each row, the categorical latent codes are the same for all the 10 images. For each column, the continuous latent codes are the same for the 10 images. For each row, we traverse/vary c_1 and c_2 from -1 to 1. We observe that InfoGAN disentangles nicely the discrete latent codes whilst HSIC-InfoGAN achieves a satisfactory level of disentanglement. When varying c_2, HSIC-InfoGAN mixes digit 0 and 8 as well as digit 3 and 5. Considering c_1 mostly captures rotation information and c_2 mostly captures thickness information, we observe that HSIC-InfoGAN learns better c_1 and similar c_2 compared to InfoGAN. Overall, HSIC-InfoGAN achieves satisfactory performance on unsupervised learning of disentangled representations. Considering the benefits of avoiding introducing auxiliary networks, HSIC-InfoGAN offers a good alternative to InfoGAN.

InfoGAN   HSIC-InfoGAN

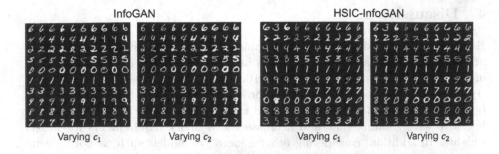

Varying c_1 Varying c_2 Varying c_1 Varying c_2

Fig. 1. Visual results from InfoGAN and HSIC-InfoGAN.

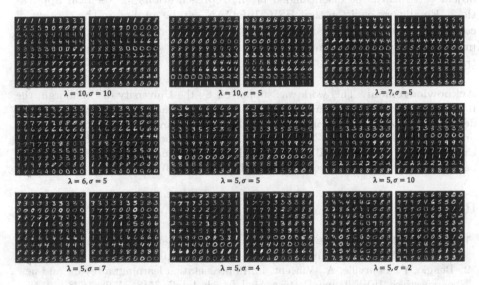

$\lambda = 10, \sigma = 10$ $\lambda = 10, \sigma = 5$ $\lambda = 7, \sigma = 5$

$\lambda = 6, \sigma = 5$ $\lambda = 5, \sigma = 5$ $\lambda = 5, \sigma = 10$

$\lambda = 5, \sigma = 7$ $\lambda = 5, \sigma = 4$ $\lambda = 5, \sigma = 2$

Fig. 2. Qualitative results of finding the optimal λ and σ for HSIC-InfoGAN.

3.3   Strategy for Hyperparameter Tuning

As we discussed in Sect. 2, the tunable hyperparameters are the HSIC loss weight λ and the kernel variance σ. We observe that it is important to ensure the generator loss and the HSIC loss have the same order of magnitude. Note that increasing λ or decreasing σ increase the HSIC loss. As shown in Fig. 2, we show the results of varying λ and σ. Changing σ causes more significant changes to the HSIC loss (roughly, we can consider that HSIC $\sim exp(-\frac{1}{\sigma^2})$). Hence, the strategy is to find a good σ first (search from $\sigma = 2$ to $\sigma = 10$ in our case) and then fine tune by finding the optimal λ.

4 Discussion

HSIC-InfoGAN could be widely used in many medical applications. As discussed in [14], many disentanglement methods in the medical domain take advantage of content-style disentanglement [4,15,16,24,25]. In this case, the content and style representations are usually a tensor and a vector [17]. HSIC-InfoGAN can be applied as an alternative to replace the (InfoGAN-style) latent regression losses to save training time and decrease the memory requirements for model weights. In addition, considering other generative models such as normalising flows [21], energy-based models [7] and denoising diffusion models [23], the HSIC loss (approximating the mutual information) could be used as an unsupervised objective to learn the disentangled latent representations for medical applications. Finally, we envision that HSIC-InfoGAN can be applied in the context of contrastive learning for medical applications [3], where one can maximise and minimise the mutual information between features of (different) images as contrastive losses.

Acknowledgement. This work was supported by the University of Edinburgh, the Royal Academy of Engineering and Canon Medical Research Europe by a PhD studentship to Xiao Liu. This work was partially supported by the Alan Turing Institute under the EPSRC grant EP/N510129/1. S.A. Tsaftaris acknowledges the support of Canon Medical and the Royal Academy of Engineering and the Research Chairs and Senior Research Fellowships scheme (grant RCSRF1819\8\25).

References

1. Belghazi, M.I., et al.: Mutual information neural estimation. In: International Conference on Machine Learning, pp. 531–540. PMLR (2018)
2. Bengio, Y., Courville, A., Vincent, P.: Representation learning: a review and new perspectives. IEEE Trans. Pattern Anal. Mach. Intell. **35**(8), 1798–1828 (2013)
3. Chaitanya, K., Erdil, E., Karani, N., Konukoglu, E.: Contrastive learning of global and local features for medical image segmentation with limited annotations. Adv. Neural. Inf. Process. Syst. **33**, 12546–12558 (2020)
4. Chartsias, A., Joyce, T., et al.: Disentangled representation learning in cardiac image analysis. Media **58**, 101535 (2019)
5. Chen, X., Duan, Y., Houthooft, R., Schulman, J., Sutskever, I., Abbeel, P.: InfoGAN: interpretable representation learning by information maximizing generative adversarial nets. In: Advances in Neural Information Processing Systems, vol. 29 (2016)
6. Cover, T.M., Thomas, J.A.: Elements of Information Theory. Wiley Interscience (2006)
7. Du, Y., Li, S., Sharma, Y., Tenenbaum, J., Mordatch, I.: Unsupervised learning of compositional energy concepts. Adv. Neural. Inf. Process. Syst. **34**, 15608–15620 (2021)
8. Goodfellow, I., et al.: Generative adversarial nets. In: Advances in Neural Information Processing Systems, vol. 27 (2014)

9. Huang, X., Liu, M.Y., Belongie, S., Kautz, J.: Multimodal unsupervised image-to-image translation. In: Proceedings of the European Conference on Computer Vision, pp. 172–189 (2018)

10. Kingma, D.P., Ba, J.: Adam: a method for stochastic optimization. In: International Conference on Learning Representations (2015)

11. Kingma, D.P., Welling, M.: Auto-encoding variational bayes. In: Proceedings of the International Conference on Learning Representations (2013)

12. LeCun, Y., Bengio, Y., Hinton, G.: Deep learning. Nature **521**(7553), 436–444 (2015)

13. LeCun, Y., Bottou, L., Bengio, Y., Haffner, P.: Gradient-based learning applied to document recognition. Proc. IEEE **86**(11), 2278–2324 (1998)

14. Liu, X., Sanchez, P., Thermos, S., O'Neil, A.Q., Tsaftaris, S.A.: Learning disentangled representations in the imaging domain. Med. Image Anal. 102516 (2022)

15. Liu, X., Thermos, S., Chartsias, A., O'Neil, A., Tsaftaris, S.A.: Disentangled representations for domain-generalized cardiac segmentation. In: Puyol Anton, E., et al. (eds.) STACOM 2020. LNCS, vol. 12592, pp. 187–195. Springer, Cham (2021). https://doi.org/10.1007/978-3-030-68107-4_19

16. Liu, X., Thermos, S., O'Neil, A., Tsaftaris, S.A.: Semi-supervised meta-learning with disentanglement for domain-generalised medical image segmentation. In: de Bruijne, M., et al. (eds.) MICCAI 2021. LNCS, vol. 12902, pp. 307–317. Springer, Cham (2021). https://doi.org/10.1007/978-3-030-87196-3_29

17. Liu, X., Thermos, S., Valvano, G., Chartsias, A., O'Neil, A., Tsaftaris, S.A.: Metrics for exposing the biases of content-style disentanglement. In: British Machine Vision Conference (2021)

18. Locatello, F., et al.: Challenging common assumptions in the unsupervised learning of disentangled representations. In: ICML, pp. 4114–4124. PMLR (2019)

19. Ma, W.D.K., Lewis, J., Kleijn, W.B.: The HSIC bottleneck: deep learning without back-propagation. In: Proceedings of the AAAI Conference on Artificial Intelligence, vol. 34, pp. 5085–5092 (2020)

20. Odena, A., Olah, C., Shlens, J.: Conditional image synthesis with auxiliary classifier GANs. In: International Conference on Machine Learning, pp. 2642–2651. PMLR (2017)

21. Papamakarios, G., Nalisnick, E.T., Rezende, D.J., Mohamed, S., Lakshminarayanan, B.: Normalizing flows for probabilistic modeling and inference. J. Mach. Learn. Res. **22**(57), 1–64 (2021)

22. Paszke, A., et al.: Pytorch: an imperative style, high-performance deep learning library. In: Advances in Neural Information Processing Systems, vol. 32 (2019)

23. Sanchez, P., Tsaftaris, S.A.: Diffusion causal models for counterfactual estimation. In: First Conference on Causal Learning and Reasoning (2021)

24. Thermos, S., Liu, X., O'Neil, A., Tsaftaris, S.A.: Controllable cardiac synthesis via disentangled anatomy arithmetic. In: de Bruijne, M., et al. (eds.) MICCAI 2021. LNCS, vol. 12903, pp. 160–170. Springer, Cham (2021). https://doi.org/10.1007/978-3-030-87199-4_15

25. Yang, J., Dvornek, N.C., Zhang, F., Chapiro, J., Lin, M.D., Duncan, J.S.: Unsupervised domain adaptation via disentangled representations: application to cross-modality liver segmentation. In: Shen, D., et al. (eds.) MICCAI 2019. LNCS, vol. 11765, pp. 255–263. Springer, Cham (2019). https://doi.org/10.1007/978-3-030-32245-8_29

26. Zhu, J.Y., et al.: Toward multimodal image-to-image translation. In: Advances in Neural Information Processing Systems, vol. 30 (2017)

Implicit Embeddings via GAN Inversion for High Resolution Chest Radiographs

Tobias Weber[1,2]([envelope]) [iD], Michael Ingrisch[2] [iD], Bernd Bischl[1] [iD],
and David Rügamer[1] [iD]

[1] Department of Statistics, LMU Munich, Munich, Germany
{tobias.weber,bernd.bischl,david.ruegamer}@stat.uni-muenchen.de
[2] Department of Radiology, University Hospital, LMU Munich, Munich, Germany
michael.ingrisch@med.uni-muenchen.de

Abstract. Generative models allow for the creation of highly realistic artificial samples, opening up promising applications in medical imaging. In this work, we propose a multi-stage encoder-based approach to invert the generator of a generative adversarial network (GAN) for high resolution chest radiographs. This gives direct access to its implicitly formed latent space, makes generative models more accessible to researchers, and enables to apply generative techniques to actual patient's images. We investigate various applications for this embedding, including image compression, disentanglement in the encoded dataset, guided image manipulation, and creation of stylized samples. We find that this type of GAN inversion is a promising research direction in the domain of chest radiograph modeling and opens up new ways to combine realistic X-ray sample synthesis with radiological image analysis.

Keywords: Generative modeling · Latent space disentanglement · Representation learning

1 Introduction

The public release of large datasets for chest radiographs has led to substantial progress in the automated analysis of thoracic X-ray imaging [19,30,40]. This availability of large amounts of data facilitates fitting complex generative models with various applications. For example, [15,34] propose an algorithm that creates deceptively real synthetic chest X-ray samples based on generative adversarial networks (GANs [13]). In this likelihood-free approach, a generator G is tasked to synthesize fake data from randomly distributed noise $z \in \mathcal{Z}$ in an adversarial setting, while a discriminator network serves as a counterpart that needs to distinguish between the real and fake data.

Previously, GANs were applied in the context of chest radiography as a generative augmentation method to increase the performance of classifiers for underrepresented pathologies [15,37]. Other applications of generative methods in this domain involve bone suppression [14,25] and creation of disease saliency maps for abnormal samples [38].

J. Fragemann et al. (Eds.): MAD 2022, LNCS 13823, pp. 22–32, 2023.
https://doi.org/10.1007/978-3-031-25046-0_3

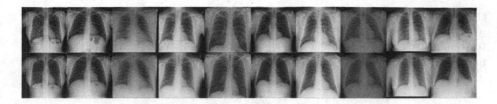

Fig. 1. ChestX-ray14 [40] samples (**top**) and their full resolution reconstructions (**bottom**) from our latent embedding by a GAN-based generator [34].

The implicitly formed latent space $\mathcal{Z}$ by GAN-based approaches has been proven to encode disentangled features of the training data with a semantic meaning [12,16,22,35]. A standard GAN model formulation, however, does not allow to access the encoded information.

One remedy for obtaining this latent code is by inverting G and directly projecting data into $\mathcal{Z}$. A possible taxonomy [4,42] of the GAN inversion topic divides approaches into three groups: 1) Learning-based variants employ an encoder to approximate the embedding [29,32,39,41]. 2) Optimization-based approaches iteratively optimize the latent code $z \in \mathcal{Z}$ for a given target image directly [1,2,7,28]. 3) Hybrid approaches combine the previously mentioned strategies and make use of the encoding as well as the optimization [3]. In the domain of medical imaging, [31] focuses on adjustable mammogram generation via embeddings in the latent space for tumor inpainting. In [11], an inverted GAN assists in converting abdominal computed tomography scans to magnetic resonance images and vice versa. In contrast, [33] apply the reverted generation process as a proxy to increase output probabilities in various target classes for explaining deep black-box classifiers.

Our Contribution. In this paper, we propose a novel multi-stage hybrid approach with bootstrapped pre-training for aligning the encoder directly to the distribution of the generator to map thoracic X-ray images into $\mathcal{Z}$. Moreover, we elaborate on practical applications and implications of this implicitly created embedding space in the domain of chest radiography on a full dataset scale. This includes the aspect of image compression (cf. Fig. 1), disentangled encoding in the latent space, and the ability to perform image manipulations beyond synthetic sample generation. Our method allows us to, e.g., model the course of thorax or lung diseases on the actual radiographs on real-world patient data, or create stylized or similar samples for a given target chest X-ray image using the reverse encoding.

2   Methods

In GANs, the generator defines a mapping $G: \mathcal{Z} \to \mathcal{X}$, where $\mathcal{X}$ is an arbitrary data space and $\mathcal{Z}$ forms the latent space. In contrast to most $\mathcal{X}$, the latent space is considered as smooth and implicitly encodes rich disentangled semantic features in a low-dimensional manifold with $\dim(\mathcal{Z}) \ll \dim(\mathcal{X})$. However, due to the nature of GAN training and the non-invertibility of neural networks, the mapping from $\mathcal{X}$ to $\mathcal{Z}$ is unknown. This problem can also be portrayed as

$$z^* = \arg\min_{z \in \mathcal{Z}} \mathcal{L}(G(z), x), \tag{1}$$

where z^* minimizes a pre-defined criterion $\mathcal{L} : \mathcal{X} \times \mathcal{X} \to \mathbb{R}$ such as the mean squared error (MSE) for $z \in \mathcal{Z}$ and $x \in \mathcal{X}$. In this work, we employ a three-stage hybrid approach to estimate the ideal latent code z^* (cf. Fig. 2).

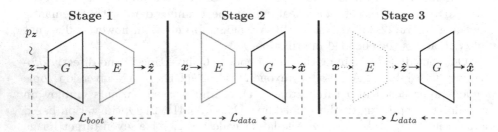

Fig. 2. Overview of our three-stage hybrid inversion approach. The red color symbolizes the part of the architecture with trainable parameters. The pre-training phase (Stage 1, **left**) learns a latent code representation of artificial samples. In Stage 2 (**middle**) the encoder E is finetuned with real data samples x. Lastly, each estimated $\hat{z} = E(x)$ is iteratively refined with frozen network components (**right**). (Color figure online)

Stage 1: Bootstrapped Training. As a first step, we use an encoder $E : \mathcal{X} \to \mathcal{Z}$ to approximate the inversion of G. To account for the limited availability of training data, we propose to exploit the generation capabilities of G by sampling z from a pre-defined distribution p_z (e.g., standard normal distribution) and producing new $x = G(z)$. This composition allows for training E on the latent code directly and on a theoretically infinite amount of data. [5] also show that z already represents compositional properties of x and a strong image prior is formed by the regressor. We define the objective for one weight update of E with a batch size of B as

$$\mathcal{L}_{boot} = \frac{1}{B} \sum_{i=1}^{B} |z_i - E(G(z_i))| \tag{2}$$

with $|\cdot|$ being the l_1 norm and $z_i \sim p_z$. We hypothesize that this bootstrapped form of pre-training leads to a better generalization of E as the generator is also able to generate meaningful edge- and out-of-distribution samples.

Stage 2: Dataset Training. In the second stage of our approach, E is finetuned on real data observations $x \in \mathcal{X}$ using the loss $\mathcal{L}_{data}$, a criterion for the distance of x and $\hat{x} = G(E(x))$. More specifically, since $\mathcal{X}$ is assumed to reside in the image domain, we employ multiple losses as in [1,39] that account for various levels of similarity: $\mathcal{L}_{MOCO}$ minimizes the angle of feature embeddings produced by a contrastive network C for true and predicted observations x and $\hat{x}$. It is defined as

$$\mathcal{L}_{MOCO} = 1 - C(x)^\mathsf{T} C(\hat{x}). \tag{3}$$

Following [39], C is a ResNet-50 [18] trained on Image-net [8] with MOCOv2 [6,17]. To enforce perceptual similarity, $\mathcal{L}_{LPIPS}$ [43] is chosen, which compares weight-scaled activations of x and $\hat{x}$ in hidden layers of a pre-trained VGG16 [36] network, i.e. it aligns deep features of original and reconstruction. Lastly, $\mathcal{L}_{MSE}$ serves as a measure for the pixel-wise distance. We combine these losses into

$$\mathcal{L}_{data} = \lambda_{MSE}\mathcal{L}_{MSE} + \lambda_{LPIPS}\mathcal{L}_{LPIPS} + \lambda_{MOCO}\mathcal{L}_{MOCO}, \tag{4}$$

where the regularization parameters $\lambda. \in \mathbb{R}^+$ are used to weigh the different losses.

Stage 3: Iterative Optimization. The area of interest in medical imaging is often only a small part of the full image. To further enhance the quality of the inversion, we utilize gradient-based per sample optimization of (1) to obtain a latent code close to z^* for selected images. Here, $z = E(x)$ and Eq. (1) is used as objective function with $\mathcal{L}_{data}$ as criterion. Note that this optimization only involves z as trainable parameter.

3   Experiments

The basis for our experiments is the ChestX-ray14 dataset [40] with over 100k images in 1024×1024 pixel resolution of 30k patients and 14 labeled pathologies. We build on the work of [34], which provides a progressive growing generator [20] for the generation of synthetic chest radiographs as G with $\dim(\mathcal{Z}) = 512$ and $p_z = \mathcal{N}(0, I)$. E utilizes ConvNext-small [26] as a backbone, where we replace the last layer with a fully connected layer, whose output dimension matches the dimension of the latent space. Stage 1 is trained with a batch size of 64 and 500k batch updates. E is then finetuned for 15 epochs on the dataset in stage 2. Both stages use the Adam [24] optimizer with learning rates of 5e−5 and 1e−5, respectively. Iterative optimization is done with 3000 iterations.

3.1   Image Compression and Quality of Reconstruction

One of the main criteria for a successful inversion is the reconstruction quality from the obtained z. In the best-case scenario, E and G enforce a cycle consistency [9,44], i.e., a perfect inversion. In Fig. 3 different examples from the test set are depicted. The inversion process captures the majority of key image features,

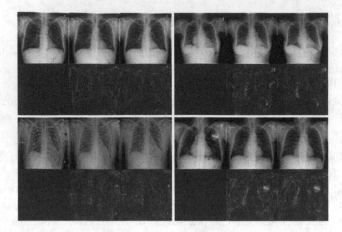

Fig. 3. Reconstruction capabilities of E. The four examples show the original image (**left** column) as well as the reconstruction from z estimated by E (**central** column) and after iterative optimization (**right** column). In each case, the **bottom row** visualizes the residual from the original with purple being a zero value and brighter values correspond to larger errors.

while the iterative optimization results in smaller residuals compared to the single encoder pass. Quantitatively, this evaluates to an increase of the structural similarity index measure from 0.813 to 0.825 and a peak signal-to-noise ratio from 22.28 to 23.95 on the test dataset. The reconstruction is bounded by the capacity of G and as stated in [34], the synthetic samples lack some details of image annotations and external medical devices like chest tubes or pacemakers. We observe that these artifacts are simply missing in the reconstructed image. In this application, GAN inversion can be understood as a special form of compression as the high-resolution input is condensed into a semantic 512-dimensional vector, which is $\approx 0.05\%$ of its original size. While compression requires additional expert knowledge to assure that all relevant information of the original images is retained in $\mathcal{Z}$, the ad-hoc identification of spurious features is another application of the inversion method and allows medical laypersons to quickly identify abnormalities in the data.

3.2   Disentanglement in Latent Space

Mapping a complex and sparse $\mathcal{X}$ to the latent $\mathcal{Z}$ results in a smooth and highly semantic representation [35], which allows for further disentanglement analysis of the radiograph's features. In particular, grouping distinctive features becomes feasible in this low-dimensional space. We use the non-linear UMAP [27] to further condense the latent code and apply density-based clustering (DBSCAN, [10]) to isolate groups, resulting in Fig. 4. Visual exploration suggests that most variation of the data stems from the sex of patients as well as the image contrast, signal intensity, and the patient's posture. These attributes mostly form coherent

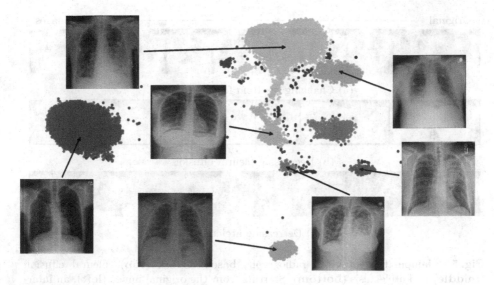

Fig. 4. UMAP embedding (point clouds) of the test set's latent code. Selected samples show key characteristics of various clusters.

clusters. An analysis of the reduced embedding based on certain pathologies proves difficult, as these are often high-frequency features with low importance for the image reconstruction and account only for minimal variation in $\mathcal{Z}$.

3.3   Guided Image Manipulation

Disentangled semantics in $\mathcal{Z}$ allow manipulating explicit features of an individual image x. We investigate the technique of InterFaceGAN [35] for facial editing applied to our use case. Based on a pre-specified target attribute, a support vector machine (SVM) with a linear kernel is trained to separate the latent codes of the dataset, which were obtained by E. The normal vector $\mathbf{n}$ of the resulting hyperplane then serves as interpolation axis and allows to generate new latent codes z_{new} along the direction of most class diversity: $z_{\text{new}} = z + \alpha\mathbf{n}$, where $\alpha \in \mathbb{R}$ is a scaling factor. By increasing α, the chosen target attribute in the generated image from z_{new} will be more pronounced and vice versa, while other features of the image remain unchanged. Figure 5 exemplarily explores the manipulation of a patient's sex, pleural effusion, and atelectasis. We observe that conditions with a large impact on the full image, such as atelectasis, pleural effusion, or cardiomegaly, are suitable for this type of manipulation. Diseases on smaller scales such as lung nodules, on the other hand, are not well captured by the latent embedding and are thus more challenging to manipulate.

Original ─────────────────────────────────→ Synthesized images

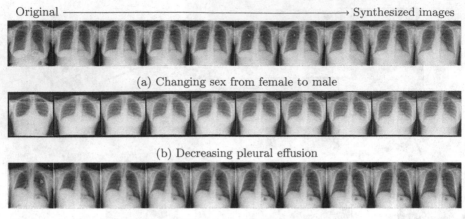

(a) Changing sex from female to male

(b) Decreasing pleural effusion

(c) Decreasing atelectasis

Fig. 5. Manipulation of given radiographs based on sex (**top**), pleural effusion (**middle**) and atelectasis (**bottom**). Starting from the original image (**left**), an interpolation along **n** shows the desired change.

3.4   Proximity Sampling

Aside from guided image manipulation, the latent embedding of a radiograph can also be used to synthesize new samples with the style and core features of its original image. This can be achieved by sampling new latent vectors in the proximity of the targeted z and reconstructing an image from the sample with G as depicted in Fig. 6. Random samples in the close neighborhood of the original image show minor variations of key features. The further the distance, the more variation is observed in the generated output image.

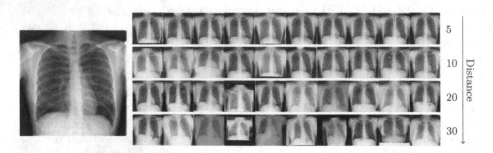

Fig. 6. Generating various samples in the neighborhood of one example scan (**left**). The **right** grid shows samples with a growing Euclidean distance to the original.

4   Outlook and Conclusion

While producing highly realistic samples, resulting images of our inversion process miss medical devices and often fine-grained details that are crucial for diagnosing pathologies. A potential solution to this could be a different backbone architecture such as current state-of-the-art style-based architectures [21–23] instead of relying on PGAN [20] as in [34]. These GAN variants do not rely on a parametric space assumption, but learn a representation $\mathcal{W}$ of $\mathcal{Z}$ using a non-linear map and allow the extension to $\mathcal{W}+$ with layer-specific latent codes in the subsequent inversion task. This results in additional out-of-distribution generalizability for better reconstruction quality and style mixing [42]. Utilizing $\mathcal{W}$ contributes to enhanced linear separability with respect to certain key features and promotes disentanglement [22], which in turn could be decisive for our classifier-based image traversing on pathologies. It could also be beneficial for future research to enlarge the training data by, e.g., incorporating the CheXpert database [19].

In this paper, we examined the capability and opportunities of GAN inversion in the context of chest radiographs. We employed a multi-stage hybrid procedure, which utilizes both an encoder and an iterative optimization to map high-resolution images to latent code. Furthermore, we have shown that GAN inversion can be used to explore the implicit latent representation of chest X-ray images, and have demonstrated applications such as data compression, disentanglement in the latent space, guided image manipulation, and synthesizing of stylized samples.

Acknowledgments. This work has been funded by the German Federal Ministry of Education and Research and the Bavarian State Ministry for Science and the Arts. The authors of this work take full responsibility for its content. The authors gratefully acknowledge LMU Klinikum for providing computing resources on their Clinical Open Research Engine (CORE). We thank the anonymous reviewers for their constructive comments, which helped us to improve the manuscript.

References

1. Abdal, R., Qin, Y., Wonka, P.: Image2StyleGAN: how to embed images into the StyleGAN latent space? In: Proceedings of the IEEE/CVF International Conference on Computer Vision, pp. 4432–4441 (2019)
2. Abdal, R., Qin, Y., Wonka, P.: Image2StyleGAN++: how to edit the embedded images? In: Proceedings of the IEEE/CVF Conference on Computer Vision and Pattern Recognition, pp. 8296–8305 (2020)
3. Bau, D., et al.: Seeing what a GAN cannot generate. In: Proceedings of the IEEE/CVF International Conference on Computer Vision, pp. 4502–4511 (2019)

4. Bermano, A.H., et al.: State-of-the-art in the architecture, methods and applications of StyleGAN. In: Computer Graphics Forum, vol. 41, pp. 591–611. Wiley Online Library (2022)
5. Chai, L., Wulff, J., Isola, P.: Using latent space regression to analyze and leverage compositionality in GANs. In: 9th International Conference on Learning Representations, ICLR (2021)
6. Chen, X., Fan, H., Girshick, R., He, K.: Improved Baselines with Momentum Contrastive Learning. arXiv:2003.04297 (2020)
7. Creswell, A., Bharath, A.A.: Inverting the generator of a generative adversarial network. IEEE Trans. Neural Netw. Learn. Syst. **30**(7), 1967–1974 (2018)
8. Deng, J., Dong, W., Socher, R., Li, L.J., Li, K., Fei-Fei, L.: ImageNet: a large-scale hierarchical image database. In: 2009 IEEE Conference on Computer Vision and Pattern Recognition, pp. 248–255. IEEE (2009)
9. Donahue, J., Krähenbühl, P., Darrell, T.: Adversarial feature learning. In: 5th International Conference on Learning Representations, ICLR (2017)
10. Ester, M., Kriegel, H.P., Sander, J., Xu, X.: A density-based algorithm for discovering clusters in large spatial databases with noise. In: Proceedings of the Second International Conference on Knowledge Discovery and Data Mining, KDD 1996, Portland, Oregon, pp. 226–231. AAAI Press (1996)
11. Fetty, L., et al.: Latent space manipulation for high-resolution medical image synthesis via the StyleGAN. Z. Med. Phys. **30**(4), 305–314 (2020)
12. Goetschalckx, L., Andonian, A., Oliva, A., Isola, P.: GANalyze: toward visual definitions of cognitive image properties. In: Proceedings of the IEEE/CVF International Conference on Computer Vision, pp. 5744–5753 (2019)
13. Goodfellow, I., et al.: Generative adversarial networks. In: Advances in Neural Information Processing Systems, vol. 27 (2014)
14. Han, L., Lyu, Y., Peng, C., Zhou, S.K.: GAN-based disentanglement learning for chest X-ray rib suppression. Med. Image Anal. **77** (2022)
15. Han, T., et al.: Breaking medical data sharing boundaries by using synthesized radiographs. Sci. Adv. **6**(49), eabb7973 (2020)
16. Härkönen, E., Hertzmann, A., Lehtinen, J., Paris, S.: GANSpace: discovering interpretable GAN controls. Adv. Neural. Inf. Process. Syst. **33**, 9841–9850 (2020)
17. He, K., Fan, H., Wu, Y., Xie, S., Girshick, R.: Momentum contrast for unsupervised visual representation learning. In: Proceedings of the IEEE/CVF Conference on Computer Vision and Pattern Recognition, pp. 9729–9738 (2020)
18. He, K., Zhang, X., Ren, S., Sun, J.: Deep residual learning for image recognition. In: Proceedings of the IEEE Conference on Computer Vision and Pattern Recognition, pp. 770–778 (2016)
19. Irvin, J., et al.: CheXpert: a large chest radiograph dataset with uncertainty labels and expert comparison. In: Proceedings of the AAAI Conference on Artificial Intelligence, vol. 33, pp. 590–597 (2019)
20. Karras, T., Aila, T., Laine, S., Lehtinen, J.: Progressive growing of GANs for improved quality, stability, and variation. In: 6th International Conference on Learning Representations, ICLR (2018)
21. Karras, T., et al.: Alias-free generative adversarial networks. In: Advances in Neural Information Processing Systems, vol. 34 (2021)
22. Karras, T., Laine, S., Aila, T.: A style-based generator architecture for generative adversarial networks. In: Proceedings of the IEEE/CVF Conference on Computer Vision and Pattern Recognition, pp. 4401–4410 (2019)

23. Karras, T., Laine, S., Aittala, M., Hellsten, J., Lehtinen, J., Aila, T.: Analyzing and improving the image quality of StyleGAN. In: Proceedings of the IEEE/CVF Conference on Computer Vision and Pattern Recognition, pp. 8110–8119 (2020)
24. Kingma, D.P., Ba, J.: Adam: a method for stochastic optimization. In: 3rd International Conference on Learning Representations, ICLR (2017)
25. Li, Z., Li, H., Han, H., Shi, G., Wang, J., Zhou, S.K.: Encoding CT anatomy knowledge for unpaired chest X-ray image decomposition. In: Shen, D., et al. (eds.) MICCAI 2019. LNCS, vol. 11769, pp. 275–283. Springer, Cham (2019). https://doi.org/10.1007/978-3-030-32226-7_31
26. Liu, Z., Mao, H., Wu, C.Y., Feichtenhofer, C., Darrell, T., Xie, S.: A ConvNet for the 2020s. arXiv:2201.03545 (2022)
27. McInnes, L., Healy, J., Saul, N., Großberger, L.: UMAP: uniform manifold approximation and projection. J. Open Source Softw. 3(29), 861 (2018)
28. Menon, S., Damian, A., Hu, S., Ravi, N., Rudin, C.: PULSE: self-supervised photo upsampling via latent space exploration of generative models. In: Proceedings of the IEEE/CVF Conference on Computer Vision and Pattern Recognition, pp. 2437–2445 (2020)
29. Nitzan, Y., Bermano, A., Li, Y., Cohen-Or, D.: Face identity disentanglement via latent space mapping. ACM Trans. Graph. 39(6), 225:1–225:14 (2020)
30. Rajpurkar, P., et al.: CheXNet: Radiologist-Level Pneumonia Detection on Chest X-Rays with Deep Learning. arXiv:1711.05225 (2017)
31. Ren, Z., Yu, S.X., Whitney, D.: Controllable medical image generation via GAN. J. Percept. Imaging 5, 000502-1–000502-15 (2022)
32. Richardson, E., et al.: Encoding in style: a StyleGAN encoder for image-to-image translation. In: Proceedings of the IEEE/CVF Conference on Computer Vision and Pattern Recognition, pp. 2287–2296 (2021)
33. Schutte, K., Moindrot, O., Hérent, P., Schiratti, J.B., Jégou, S.: Using StyleGAN for Visual Interpretability of Deep Learning Models on Medical Images. arXiv:2101.07563 (2021)
34. Segal, B., Rubin, D.M., Rubin, G., Pantanowitz, A.: Evaluating the clinical realism of synthetic chest X-rays generated using progressively growing GANs. SN Comput. Sci. 2(4), 1–17 (2021). https://doi.org/10.1007/s42979-021-00720-7
35. Shen, Y., Gu, J., Tang, X., Zhou, B.: Interpreting the latent space of GANs for semantic face editing. In: Proceedings of the IEEE/CVF Conference on Computer Vision and Pattern Recognition, pp. 9243–9252 (2020)
36. Simonyan, K., Zisserman, A.: Very deep convolutional networks for large-scale image recognition. In: 3rd International Conference on Learning Representations, ICLR (2015)
37. Sundaram, S., Hulkund, N.: GAN-based data augmentation for chest X-ray classification. arXiv:2107.02970 (2021)
38. Tang, Y., Tang, Y., Zhu, Y., Xiao, J., Summers, R.M.: A disentangled generative model for disease decomposition in chest X-rays via normal image synthesis. Med. Image Anal. 67 (2021)
39. Tov, O., Alaluf, Y., Nitzan, Y., Patashnik, O., Cohen-Or, D.: Designing an encoder for StyleGAN image manipulation. ACM Trans. Graph. (TOG) 40(4), 1–14 (2021)
40. Wang, X., Peng, Y., Lu, L., Lu, Z., Bagheri, M., Summers, R.M.: Chestx-ray8: hospital-scale chest X-ray database and benchmarks on weakly-supervised classification and localization of common thorax diseases. In: Proceedings of the IEEE Conference on Computer Vision and Pattern Recognition, pp. 2097–2106 (2017)
41. Wei, T., et al.: E2Style: improve the efficiency and effectiveness of StyleGAN inversion. IEEE Trans. Image Process. 31, 3267–3280 (2022)

42. Xia, W., Zhang, Y., Yang, Y., Xue, J.H., Zhou, B., Yang, M.H.: GAN Inversion: A Survey. arXiv:2101.05278 (2022)
43. Zhang, R., Isola, P., Efros, A.A., Shechtman, E., Wang, O.: The unreasonable effectiveness of deep features as a perceptual metric. In: Proceedings of the IEEE Conference on Computer Vision and Pattern Recognition, pp. 586–595 (2018)
44. Zhu, J.Y., Park, T., Isola, P., Efros, A.A.: Unpaired image-to-image translation using cycle-consistent adversarial networks. In: Proceedings of the IEEE International Conference on Computer Vision, pp. 2223–2232 (2017)

Disentangled Representation Learning for Privacy-Preserving Case-Based Explanations

Helena Montenegro[1,2]([✉]), Wilson Silva[1,2], and Jaime S. Cardoso[1,2]

[1] Faculty of Engineering, University of Porto, Porto, Portugal
up201604184@edu.fe.up.pt
[2] INESC TEC, Porto, Portugal

Abstract. The lack of interpretability of Deep Learning models hinders their deployment in clinical contexts. Case-based explanations can be used to justify these models' decisions and improve their trustworthiness. However, providing medical cases as explanations may threaten the privacy of patients. We propose a generative adversarial network to disentangle identity and medical features from images. Using this network, we can alter the identity of an image to anonymize it while preserving relevant explanatory features. As a proof of concept, we apply the proposed model to biometric and medical datasets, demonstrating its capacity to anonymize medical images while preserving explanatory evidence and a reasonable level of intelligibility. Finally, we demonstrate that the model is inherently capable of generating counterfactual explanations.

Keywords: Case-based explanations · Image anonymization · Medical image analysis · Generative adversarial networks · Causality

1 Introduction

Deep Learning models are often misguided by spurious correlations in the data that do not exist in the real world, leading models with good test performance to fail when deployed into real contexts [5,16]. Interpretability is imperative to trust and accept Deep Learning models in the medical scene. Among the existing interpretability techniques, case-based explanations provide intuitive insights into a models' reasoning by showing similar examples from the data [15]. However, the use of medical images as explanations raises privacy concerns.

The use of case-based explanations in clinical contexts requires that these explanations go through an anonymization process that alters their identity-related characteristics while preserving their medical content and intelligibility [19,20]. The current literature on anonymizing images [3,4,7,9,21,27] is insufficient since most methods do not consider the explicit preservation of explanatory features in the images, which compromises their value as case-based explanations. Only one method considers the use of the anonymized images as case-based explanations and, thus, the explicit preservation of explanatory evidence [18].

J. Fragemann et al. (Eds.): MAD 2022, LNCS 13823, pp. 33–45, 2023.
https://doi.org/10.1007/978-3-031-25046-0_4

The process of anonymizing an image while maintaining its intelligibility implies manufacturing a new identity for the anonymized image that is sufficiently different from the identities of patients in the dataset so that none of them can be recognized. The model proposed in [18] anonymizes images by implicitly creating a new identity that cannot be recognized by identity recognition networks. However, it does not explicitly disentangle identity and medical features. As such, it might preserve identity features closely related to the preserved medical features. Furthermore, it is impossible to control the identity manufactured for the anonymized images in the model.

In this work, we address the weaknesses of the literature by proposing a privacy-preserving generative model inspired by causality [22] that explicitly disentangles medical and identity features. The model contains three modules organized according to the causal graph in Fig. 1. In this graph, disease and identity are two independent modules causally-related to the image. Using the proposed model, we can make interventions on an image's identity to anonymize it. Furthermore, we can easily make interventions to its disease to obtain counterfactual explanations. We apply our model to a biometric dataset of eye iris images (Warsaw-BioBase-Disease-v2.1) [24–26], to verify its capacity to anonymize images with well-defined identity features. Moreover, we apply the model to medical data of chest radiographs (CheXpert) [12,13], to assess its capacity to preserve medical features during the anonymization process.

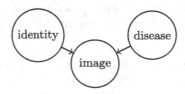

Fig. 1. Causal graph describing relationships between the network's modules.

2   Related Work

This section analyses the related work in image anonymization techniques, considering their application to medical case-based explanations. Additionally, it presents background on relevant deep generative models.

2.1   Image Anonymization

Traditional image anonymization methods, like blurring and the K-Same-based methods [9], are applied over the whole input image. Deep Learning methods can automatically identify the regions of the images that discriminate identity using identity recognition networks, and alter them using deep generative models. Most Deep Learning methods [3,4,7,21,27] do not explicitly preserve the relevant task-related features of the original image, which constitute explanatory evidence in the context of explanations.

The only work from the literature that considers the use of the privacy-preserving images as explanations is [18], as it addresses the explicit preservation of explanatory features. The generative model proposed in [18] uses identity recognition networks to promote that the generated images are sufficiently different from the training data as to not disclose the identity of any patient. This method preserves explanatory evidence by reconstructing the disease-related features of the original images, obtained through saliency maps, in their anonymized versions. Saliency maps expose the location and intensity of the disease-related features in an image. As such, their application to reconstruct disease-related features preserves the absolute position of the features, disregarding the possibility that the position of these features could change in accordance with the alterations to the structure of the body part that occur during anonymization. For example, considering the use of an eye image for glaucoma recognition, if the region of the eye that discriminates glaucoma is inside the pupil, an eye where the pupil becomes larger during anonymization should display a larger region of glaucoma-related features. As such, the preservation of explanatory evidence should not preserve the absolute position of the disease in the image, but its relative position in relation to the structure of the patient's body.

Another weakness in [18] is that the model does not disentangle identity features from explanatory features. As such, it is not possible to control the identity of the anonymized image. Moreover, as disease-related features and identity features may be entangled, by reconstructing the saliency maps of disease-related features, the model may be preserving some identity-related features closely related with the disease.

In our proposed method, we explicitly disentangle the identity and the disease in an image. As such, we can control the identity and medical content in an image by changing the inputs of the network. With this model, we can alter the identity of the images to anonymize them while preserving explanatory features. Additionally, we can generate counterfactual explanations by altering the medical content of the images.

2.2 Deep Generative Models

Generative models model the probability distribution of the data and use it to generate new data samples. The most relevant generative models for this work are Generative Adversarial Networks (GANs) and Variational Autoencoders (VAEs).

GANs [8] capture the data distribution implicitly, through two adversarial networks: a generator and a discriminator. The discriminator is a binary classification network that distinguishes between real and fake images. The generator is trained to generate realistic images, tricking the discriminator into misclassifying them as real. In the proposed method, we use GANs to generate privacy-preserving images.

VAEs [14] explicitly learn an approximation of the data distribution, which can be used to sample new data points. A VAE is composed of two networks: an encoder and a decoder. The encoder transforms an image from the original data space into its representation in a latent space with a simpler distribution.

The decoder learns to transform samples from the latent space into the original data space by reconstructing the original image from its representation. In the proposed method, we use a VAE to train an identity recognition network to extract identity features into a data space with a Gaussian distribution.

3   Proposed Methodology

We propose a generative adversarial network to anonymize images while preserving relevant explanatory features. The model, exposed in Fig. 2, uses a medical feature extractor to extract medical features from the original image. We input these medical features along with a vector of random noise to a generative adversarial network, producing an anonymized image. The vector of random noise controls the identity represented in the generated image. To promote realism in the image, we apply a realism loss obtained with a discriminator which classifies images as real or fake. To promote the association between the input noise and the generated image's identity, we minimize the distance between identity features extracted from the generated image and the input noise. Finally, to preserve the medical features of the original image, we minimize the distance between the features of the original image and of the generated image.

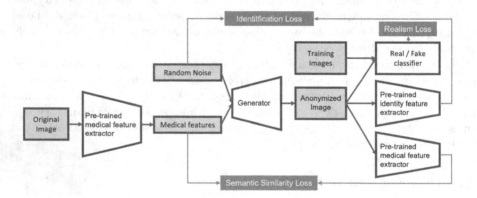

Fig. 2. Architecture of the privacy-preserving generative adversarial network.

The model is composed of three modules, which will be described in the following sections:

- **Generative Module**: composed of the generative adversarial network responsible for the generation of the anonymized image.
- **Identity Module**: composed of the identity feature extractor, which promotes the association between the vector of random noise provided to the generative network and the identity of the output image.
- **Explanatory Module**: composed of the medical feature extractor, which promotes the preservation of explanatory evidence in the anonymized image.

The model is trained in two stages. First, we train an identity recognition network and a disease recognition network to obtain the identity and medical feature extractors, respectively. Then, the generative adversarial network is trained, using the pre-trained identity and medical feature extractors to calculate its loss. The following sections describe the existing modules in detail.

3.1 Generative Module

The generative module, composed of the generator and real/fake classifier, is responsible for the generation of realistic images. To avoid problems like mode collapse, often seen during the training of GANs, we use as the generative model a Wasserstein GAN with Gradient Penalty (WGAN-GP) [10]. The discriminator D is trained to minimize the loss in Eq. 1, where X represents random noise sampled from a Gaussian distribution, p_d is the probability distribution of the images I, $\hat{x}$ corresponds to random samples, F_{exp} is the medical feature extractor, and λ is the non-negative weight assigned to the gradient penalty term.

$$\mathcal{L}_D = E_{I \sim p_d(I), X \sim N(0,1)}[D(G(X, F_{exp}(I))) - D(I)] + \\ E_{\hat{x} \sim p_{\hat{x}}}[\lambda(||\nabla_{\hat{x}} D(\hat{x})||_2 - 1)^2] \tag{1}$$

The loss function minimized by the generator G, defined in Eq. 2, is composed of three loss terms which promote that the images are realistic, that the identity represented in the anonymized image is provided by the input vector of random noise, and that the medical features of the anonymized image are similar to those of the original image. In this equation, X represents random noise, p_d is the probability distribution of the images I, λ_x are non-negative parameters used to calibrate the relevance of each loss term x, D is the discriminator, F_{exp} is the medical feature extractor, and F_{id} is the identity feature extractor.

$$\mathcal{L}_G = E_{I \sim p_d(I), X \sim N(0,1)}[-\lambda_{real} D(G(X, F_{exp}(I))) + \\ \lambda_{id}(F_{id}(G(X, F_{exp}(I))) - X)^2 + \lambda_{exp}(F_{exp}(G(X, F_{exp}(I))) - F_{exp}(I))^2] \tag{2}$$

3.2 Identity Module

The identity module is responsible for promoting the association between the random noise inputted to the generative model and the generated image's identity. This module contains a disease-invariant identity feature extractor, which is applied over the generated image to obtain its identity features and calculate the identification loss term in Eq. 2. The identity feature extractor is trained independently from the generative network.

The random noise vector must follow the same probability distribution as the extracted identity features. As such, we train the identity feature extractor as part of a Variational Autoencoder (VAE) to obtain features with a Gaussian distribution. An overview of this model is shown in Fig. 3. It contains an encoder, which extracts identity features from an image, and a decoder that reconstructs the image from its features. A multiclass identity recognition network promotes that the features can be used to identify a patient. Finally, a disease recognition network promotes that these features do not possess medical information. The loss function used to train this network is described in Eq. 3. In this equation, KL is the Kullback-Leibler divergence, C_{id} and C_{dis} are the identity and disease recognition networks, respectively, y_{id} and y_{dis} are the ground-truth labels of the images in regards to identity and disease recognition, respectively, and F_{id} is the identity feature extractor.

$$\mathcal{L}_{F_{id}} = E_{I \sim p_d(I)}[\lambda_{reg}KL(F_{id}(I)\|N(0,1)) + \lambda_{rec}(D_{id}(F_{id}(I)) - I)^2$$
$$- \lambda_{mid}y_{id}\log(C_{id}(F_{id}(I))) + \lambda_{dis}C_{dis}(F_{id}(I))\log(C_{dis}(F_{id}(I)))] \quad (3)$$

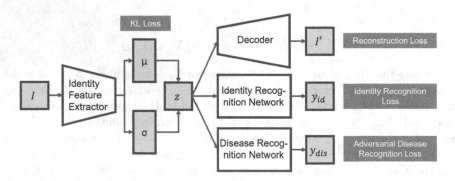

Fig. 3. Architecture of the disease-invariant identity recognition network.

In medical datasets, there may not be enough images per patient to train a multiclass identity recognition network. As such, the identity recognition network can also be trained as a Siamese network [2], using a contrastive loss [11] to increase the distance between the latent representations of images from different patients and decrease this distance between images of the same patient. The loss function of the disease-invariant identity recognition network in such cases is shown in Eq. 4.

$$\mathcal{L}_{F_{id}} = E_{I \sim p_d(I)}[\lambda_{reg}KL(F_{id}(I)\|N(0,1)) + \lambda_{rec}(D_{id}(F_{id}(I)) - I)^2$$
$$+ \lambda_{mid}(y_{id}F_{id}(I)^2 + (1 - y_{id})\max(0, (1 - F_{id}(I))^2)) \quad (4)$$
$$+ \lambda_{dis}C_{dis}(F_{id}(I))\log(C_{dis}(F_{id}(I)))]$$

3.3 Explanatory Module

The explanatory module is responsible for preserving the medical features that serve as explanatory evidence in the anonymized images. This module is composed of a medical feature extractor, which obtains the medical features that are provided as input to the generative model. We train the medical feature extractor as part of an identity-invariant disease recognition network, inspired by the work of Ghimire *et al.* [6], which presents a method based on adversarial training to train a classification network to be invariant to the source of the data. The disease recognition network contains a medical feature extractor whose features can be used by a disease classifier to recognize the disease of the image, and cannot be used by an adversarial identity classifier to identify the patient. Its loss function is defined in Eq. 5, where F_{exp} is the medical feature extractor.

$$\mathcal{L}_{F_{dis}} = E_{I \sim p_d(I)} [-y_{dis} \log(C_{dis}(F_{exp}(I))) + y_{id} \log(C_{id}(F_{exp}(I)))] \qquad (5)$$

4 Experiments and Results

In this section, we present the experiments developed to evaluate the performance of the proposed model. We used two datasets to validate the model:

- **Warsaw-BioBase-Disease-Iris v2.1** [24, 26]: contains 1,795 grayscale eye iris images from 115 different patients. The images are annotated for various eye conditions, including glaucoma. We focus on glaucoma recognition, for which the dataset is imbalanced, with only 24% of the images containing glaucoma. We split the data into 65% for training, 15% for validation and 20% for testing.
- **CheXpert** [12, 13]: contains 224,316 chest radiographs from 65,240 patients. We focus on the recognition of Pleural Effusion. We only consider 1,000 images from 592 different patients, using 75% for training, 10% for validation, and 15% for testing. The selected set of images is balanced for the recognition of Pleural Effusion.

4.1 Identity Recognition and Disease Recognition

This section measures the performance of the identity and disease recognition networks, when applied to the test data. For the iris data, we train the identity recognition network considering a multiclass classification problem with 115 classes. For the chest data, as there is a significantly higher number of patients, we train the identity recognition network as a Siamese network, considering a binary classification problem where pairs of images are classified as belonging to the same or different identities. Each test image was randomly paired with an image from the same patient and from a different patient. The empirically selected parameters used to train the identity recognition networks were: $\lambda_{reg} = 0.01$, $\lambda_{rec} = 0.01$, $\lambda_{mid} = 1$, and $\lambda_{dis} = 1$. Table 1 exposes the results.

Table 1. Results of the identity and disease recognition networks.

Data	Model	Identity R. Accuracy	Disease R. Accuracy	Disease R. F-score
Iris data	Identity recognition	74.12%	71.76%	0.00%
	Glaucoma recognition	4.41%	92.94%	87.23%
Chest data	Identity recognition	64.62%	51.49%	7.59%
	Pleural effusion recognition	50.00%	86.05%	86.54%

Table 2. Results of providing the original identity features as input to the model.

Setting	Identity recognition accuracy	Disease recognition Accuracy	F-score
Iris data ($\lambda_{exp} = 3$, $\lambda_{id} = 5$)	55.00%	87.65%	75.86%
Chest data ($\lambda_{exp} = 5$, $\lambda_{id} = 15$)	55.00%	78.74%	81.61%

The results show that the disease recognition networks are capable of extracting features that contain the medical content of the images, achieving high accuracy and F-score in disease recognition. Furthermore, the medical features are identity-invariant, as suggested by the respective low identity recognition accuracy. The identity recognition networks also show their capacity to obtain disease-invariant features, as shown by the low F-scores in disease recognition. The relatively low accuracy in identity recognition in the chest data (64.62% accuracy in a balanced binary classification setting) suggests that the task of identifying a patient in chest radiographs is difficult.

4.2 Image Anonymization

This section presents the results of the generative model, trained for 1,500 and 1,440 epochs, for the iris and chest data, respectively. In all experiments, we used $\lambda_r = 0.4$. The values of λ_{id} and λ_{exp} vary in the different experiments.

First, we evaluate the generative models' capacity to associate random noise with identity by providing the identity features of the original image as input, instead of the random noise provided during training. In this setting, we expect to obtain images similar to the original ones, as they should contain the identity and medical features of the input images. The results are shown in Table 2. The networks achieve high accuracy at identifying the original patient in the images, when compared with their baseline accuracy (Table 1). The generated images, shown in the second row of Fig. 4, are very similar to the original images in the first row. These results suggest that, during training, the network successfully learns to associate the input noise to the identity of the generated image.

In the next experiment, we use the model to generate anonymized images by providing random noise and the medical features of the original image as its inputs. The results are presented in Table 3. To evaluate the results regarding privacy, we measure the accuracy of the identity recognition networks at recognizing the identity of the original image. We also measure the average maximum

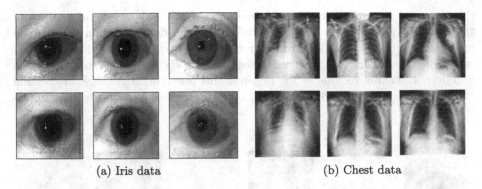

(a) Iris data   (b) Chest data

Fig. 4. Example of generated images when we provide the identity features of the original images as input to the generative model. The first row contains the original images, and the second row contains the generated images.

probability assigned by the identity recognition network to any identity in the data. In addition to the results of the anonymization models proposed in this work, Table 3 also provides the results of the identity-invariant disease recognition and disease-invariant identity recognition networks on anonymized images obtained using the privacy-preserving model with Siamese identity recognition (PP-SIR) from [18] on the iris data.

Table 3. Results of image anonymization.

Model	Identity recognition		Disease recognition	
	Accuracy	Max Avg Score	Accuracy	F-score
Iris data ($\lambda_{exp} = 3$, $\lambda_{id} = 5$)	0.88%	13.22%	87.06%	75.82%
Iris data (PP-SIR from [18])	1.18%	2.09%	74.71%	57.84%
Chest data ($\lambda_{exp} = 5$, $\lambda_{id} = 5$)	37.33%	51.16%	79.40%	82.08%

The low accuracy and maximum average score suggest that the images obtained with the proposed anonymization models are anonymized, since the identity recognition model has difficulty recognizing any identity from the data. The disease-related class of the images is preserved in their anonymized versions. When comparing our proposed model with PP-SIR, we verify that PP-SIR has a higher capacity to generate unrecognizable images, as can be seen in its lower maximum average score. However, the PP-SIR model fails at preserving identity-invariant disease-related features, unlike the proposed model which achieves significantly higher accuracy and F-score in disease recognition.

Figure 5 shows examples of results. In addition to the original and anonymized images, obtained through the proposed network, we also provide saliency maps that highlight medical features in the images. The saliency maps were obtained by applying Deep Taylor [17] to the medical feature extractor, using the implementation provided by iNNvestigate [1]. The results suggest that the proposed network has difficulty generating intelligible chest radiographs in the presence of pleural effusion. Since the iris images do not contain well-defined medical features, it is difficult to observe whether explanatory evidence is preserved in the saliency maps. Nevertheless, the saliency maps in the chest data highlight the same regions of the original and anonymized images, suggesting that the medical features of the original images are preserved during anonymization.

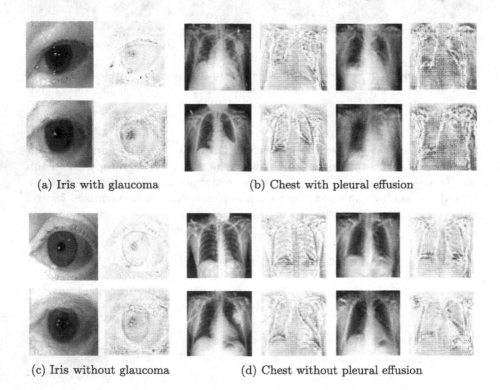

(a) Iris with glaucoma   (b) Chest with pleural effusion

(c) Iris without glaucoma   (d) Chest without pleural effusion

Fig. 5. Example of anonymized images and saliency maps highlighting disease-related features. In the iris data, the first and second rows contain the original and generated images, respectively. In the chest data, the first two columns refer to the original images, and the last two columns refer to the generated images.

4.3   Generation of Counterfactual Explanations

We apply the proposed model to the generation of counterfactual explanations, by making alterations to the medical features of the images. To do so, we provide the medical features of a randomly selected image with a different pathology than the original one as input to the generative model, along with the identity features of the original image. The model succeeds at altering the disease-related class of the original images with an accuracy of 71.18% and 77.00%, for the iris and chest data, respectively. Figure 6 shows the results.

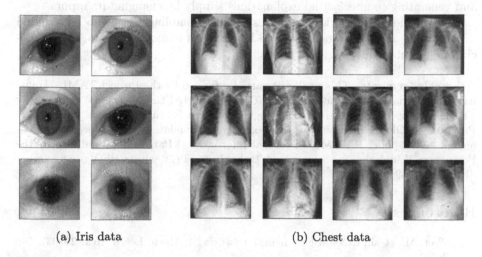

(a) Iris data   (b) Chest data

Fig. 6. Example of counterfactual explanations. The first row contains the original images, the second row contains the images from which the medical features were extracted, and the third row contains the counterfactual explanations.

Since the iris data does not contain well-defined medical features, it is difficult to analyze the quality of the respective counterfactual explanations. In the chest data, the counterfactual examples contain the disease-related features of the images in the second row, whose pathology differs from the original images in the first row.

5   Conclusions

We developed a novel privacy-preserving generative adversarial network, which disentangles identity and medical features. The experiments demonstrated that this network successfully alters the identity in an image while preserving explanatory evidence. The generated images achieved a decent level of intelligibility, generally speaking. Nonetheless, there are still cases where the proposed method has difficulty generating realistic images, namely in chest radiographs with pleural effusion. As such, future work should consider improving the generative network to increase the intelligibility of the images.

The model was applied to the generation of counterfactual explanations by altering the medical features of the images. However, since these features are not interpretable, it is difficult to make meaningful alterations. In future work, the medical feature extractor should be extended as a causal model [23] where it is possible to make interventions on tangible features causally-related to the disease to generate high-quality counterfactual explanations.

Integrating causality in the anonymization of case-based explanations leads to a simple and powerful model simultaneously capable of anonymizing images and generating counterfactual explanations simply by changing its inputs.

To conclude, this work contributes towards enabling the use of case-based explanations and, consequently, Deep Learning in clinical contexts, to aid specialists in ambiguous diagnostic cases.

Acknowledgements. This work was partially funded by the Project TAMI - Transparent Artificial Medical Intelligence (NORTE-01-0247-FEDER-045905) financed by ERDF - European Regional Fund through the North Portugal Regional Operational Program - NORTE 2020 and by the Portuguese Foundation for Science and Technology - FCT under the CMU - Portugal International Partnership, and also by the Portuguese Foundation for Science and Technology - FCT within PhD grant number SFRH/BD/139468/2018.

References

1. Alber, M., et al.: iNNvestigate neural networks! J. Mach. Learn. Res. **20**(93), 1–8 (2019)
2. Bromley, J., et al.: Signature verification using a "siamese" time delay neural network. Int. J. Pattern Recognit. Artif. Intell. **7**, 25 (1993). https://doi.org/10.1142/S0218001493000339
3. Chen, J., Konrad, J., Ishwar, P.: VGAN-based image representation learning for privacy-preserving facial expression recognition. In: CVPR, CV-COPS (2018)
4. Cho, D., Lee, J.H., Suh, I.H.: CLEANIR: controllable attribute-preserving natural identity remover. Appl. Sci. **10**(3), 1120 (2020)
5. DeGrave, A.J., Janizek, J.D., Lee, S.: AI for radiographic COVID-19 detection selects shortcuts over signal. Nat. Mach. Intell. **3**(7), 610–619 (2021)
6. Ghimire, S., Kashyap, S., Wu, J.T., Karargyris, A., Moradi, M.: Learning invariant feature representation to improve generalization across chest x-ray datasets. In: Machine Learning in Medical Imaging, pp. 644–653 (2020)
7. Gong, M., Liu, J., Li, H., Xie, Y., Tang, Z.: Disentangled representation learning for multiple attributes preserving face deidentification. IEEE Trans. Neural Netw. Learn. Syst. 1–13 (2020). https://doi.org/10.1109/TNNLS.2020.3027617
8. Goodfellow, I., et al.: Generative adversarial nets. In: Advances in Neural Information Processing Systems, vol. 27, pp. 2672–2680 (2014)
9. Gross, R., Airoldi, E., Malin, B., Sweeney, L.: Integrating utility into face de-identification. In: Danezis, G., Martin, D. (eds.) PET 2005. LNCS, vol. 3856, pp. 227–242. Springer, Heidelberg (2006). https://doi.org/10.1007/11767831_15
10. Gulrajani, I., Ahmed, F., Arjovsky, M., Dumoulin, V., Courville, A.: Improved training of Wasserstein GANs. In: NIPS 2017, pp. 5769–5779 (2017)
11. Hadsell, R., Chopra, S., LeCun, Y.: Dimensionality reduction by learning an invariant mapping. In: 2006 IEEE Computer Society Conference on Computer Vision and Pattern Recognition (CVPR 2006), vol. 2, pp. 1735–1742 (2006). https://doi.org/10.1109/CVPR.2006.100
12. Irvin, J., et al.: Chexpert: a large chest radiograph dataset with uncertainty labels and expert comparison (2019)

13. Irvin, J., et al.: Chexpert: a large chest X-ray dataset and competition (2019). https://stanfordmlgroup.github.io/competitions/chexpert/. Accessed 21 Feb 2022
14. Kingma, D.P., Welling, M.: Auto-encoding variational bayes. In: ICLR (2013)
15. Lipton, Z.C.: The mythos of model interpretability: in machine learning, the concept of interpretability is both important and slippery. Queue **16**(3), 31–57 (2018)
16. Mahmood, U., et al.: Detecting spurious correlations with sanity tests for artificial intelligence guided radiology systems. Front. Digit. Health **3**, 85 (2021)
17. Montavon, G., Lapuschkin, S., Binder, A., Samek, W., Müller, K.: Explaining nonlinear classification decisions with deep taylor decomposition. Pattern Recog. **65**, 211–222 (2017)
18. Montenegro, H., Silva, W., Cardoso, J.S.: Privacy-preserving generative adversarial network for case-based explainability in medical image analysis. IEEE Access **9**, 148037–148047 (2021)
19. Montenegro, H., Silva, W., Cardoso, J.S.: Towards privacy-preserving explanations in medical image analysis. In: IMLH Workshop, at ICML 2021 (2021)
20. Montenegro, H., Silva, W., Gaudio, A., Fredrikson, M., Smailagic, A., Cardoso, J.S.: Privacy-preserving case-based explanations: enabling visual interpretability by protecting privacy. IEEE Access **10**, 28333–28347 (2022). https://doi.org/10.1109/ACCESS.2022.3157589
21. Oleszkiewicz, W., Kairouz, P., Piczak, K., Rajagopal, R., Trzciński, T.: Siamese generative adversarial privatizer for biometric data. In: Jawahar, C.V., Li, H., Mori, G., Schindler, K. (eds.) ACCV 2018. LNCS, vol. 11365, pp. 482–497. Springer, Cham (2019). https://doi.org/10.1007/978-3-030-20873-8_31
22. Schölkopf, B.: Causality for machine learning. arXiv preprint arXiv:1911.10500 (2019)
23. Schölkopf, B., et al.: Towards causal representation learning (2021). https://doi.org/10.48550/ARXIV.2102.11107. https://arxiv.org/abs/2102.11107
24. Trokielewicz, M., Czajka, A., Maciejewicz, P.: Assessment of iris recognition reliability for eyes affected by ocular pathologies. In: BTAS Conference, pp. 1–6 (2015)
25. Trokielewicz, M., Czajka, A., Maciejewicz, P.: Biometric databases (2015). http://zbum.ia.pw.edu.pl/EN/node/46. Accessed 18 Oct 2021
26. Trokielewicz, M., Czajka, A., Maciejewicz, P.: Implications of ocular pathologies for iris recognition reliability. Image Vis. Comput. **58**, 158–167 (2017)
27. Wu, Y., Yang, F., Xu, Y., Ling, H.: Privacy-protective-GAN for privacy preserving face de-identification. J. Comput. Sci. Technol. **34**(1), 47–60 (2019). https://doi.org/10.1007/s11390-019-1898-8

Autoencoder-Based Approaches

Instance-Specific Augmentation of Brain MRIs with Variational Autoencoders

Jon Middleton[1,2,3]($\boxtimes$), Marko Bauer[1,2], Jacob Johansen[1,2,3], Mads Nielsen[1,2,3], Stefan Sommer[1,3], and Akshay Pai[2]

[1] Department of Computer Science, University of Copenhagen, Copenhagen, Denmark
{jami,mb,jj,madsn,sommer}@di.ku.dk
[2] Cerebriu A/S, Copenhagen, Denmark
ap@cerebriu.com
[3] Pioneer Centre for AI, Copenhagen, Denmark

Abstract. Spatial data augmentation is a standard technique for regularizing deep segmentation networks that are tasked with localizing medical abnormalities. However, a typical spatial augmentation scheme is built upon ad hoc selections of spatial transformation parameters which are not determined by the data set and therefore may not capture spatial variations in the data. For segmentation networks trained in the low-data regime, these ad hoc transformation techniques often fail to encourage better generalization. To address this problem, we propose a variational autoencoder framework for spatial data augmentation. We show how this framework provides a natural, data-driven approach to probabilistic, instance-specific spatial augmentation. Further, we observe that U-Nets trained on data augmented using this framework compare favorably with U-Nets trained using standard spatial augmentation methods.

Keywords: Segmentation · Disentanglement · Data augmentation · Variational autoencoders

1 Introduction

The segmentation of abnormalities of the human brain, such as strokes, tumors, and multiple sclerosis, is a major challenge in medical image analysis. Deep segmentation networks continue to demonstrate their effectiveness in localizing pathological tissue, but due to the scarcity of high-quality annotated samples, these networks tend to be trained on small data sets, leading to overfitting. Abnormality segmentation is particularly difficult, because the task demands that an algorithm distinguish an enormous variety of pathological cases from healthy tissue. Even when restricting to a single abnormality class, the large diversity of shapes and appearances means that some amount of over-fitting is inevitable. Thus, practitioners continue to seek methods for regularizing segmentation networks trained in the low-data regime.

Among the many techniques of enlarging a data set is *spatial data augmentation*, where the point elements of an image are rearranged to produce new images.

J. Fragemann et al. (Eds.): MAD 2022, LNCS 13823, pp. 49–58, 2023.
https://doi.org/10.1007/978-3-031-25046-0_5

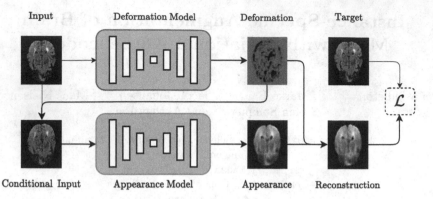

Fig. 1. Stage one of the proposed augmentation scheme. In the first stage, we use the Variationally Inferred Transformational Autoencoder framework (VITAE) in [3] to construct a deformation model. VITAE is trained to minimize a loss function $\mathcal{L}$ which incorporates a registration loss term. Backpropagation occurs along the bold arrows.

Classical methods typically use transformations from the affine group or elastic deformations. However, these synthetic deformations can be unrealistic and uninformative of the data. Recent augmentation pipelines rely on deformation models that exploit data sets to compute non-linear transformations. These approaches either rely on the template-based VoxelMorph architecture [1,11,13,23] or avoid neural networks entirely when calculating statistical deformation models [12]. Autoencoder frameworks can generate non-linear transformations using latent space disentanglement and can produce these transformations without a template image [17,20]. These techniques provide deformations in an unsupervised manner, but since the autoencoders are not variational, they do not provide a probabilistic augmentation pipeline. A Bayesian spatial augmentation approach is featured in [15], but the pipeline is adapted for augmenting classification networks.

Inspired by variational autoencoder frameworks that incorporate explicit spatial disentanglement [2,3], we present an unsupervised data augmentation scheme which learns spatial transformations based on shape variation within a data set without using templates. In particular, we contribute the following:

1. A variational autoencoder framework that produces a probabilistic spatial transformer using explicit spatial disentanglement
2. An application of probabilistic spatial transformers to training abnormality segmentation networks
3. Favorable comparisons of the proposed augmentation set up against existing augmentation methods.

2   Methods

Given a brain MRI, the task is to localize abnormal tissue using a deep segmentation network. In this section we describe a variational autoencoder framework

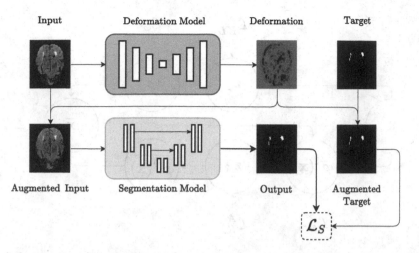

Fig. 2. Stage two of the proposed augmentation scheme. In the second stage, we train a segmentation model on data augmented by a deformation model obtained from stage one. The deformation model augments data with instance-specific spatial transformations. Errors from the segmentation loss function $\mathcal{L}_S$ backpropagate through only the segmentation network.

that contains a probabilistic spatial transformer which can augment training data for this segmentation network.

2.1   Disentangling Shape from Appearance

Variational Autoencoders. A variational autoencoder (VAE) uses a neural network to parametrize a latent variable model $p_\theta(\mathbf{z}, \mathbf{x}) = p_\theta(\mathbf{z})p_\theta(\mathbf{x}|\mathbf{z})$, where θ is the model's parameters and $\mathbf{z}$ is interpreted as a collection of low-dimensional features that are relevant for constructing high-dimensional data $\mathbf{x}$ [7]. The prior $p_\theta(\mathbf{z})$ is typically the standard normal distribution. The posterior distribution $p_\theta(\mathbf{z}|\mathbf{x})$ is interpreted as a way to encode inputs to low-dimensional features. Since $p_\theta(\mathbf{z}|\mathbf{x})$ generally has no closed form solution, it is approximated by $q_\phi(\mathbf{z}|\mathbf{x})$, where the parameters ϕ correspond to a neural network. The composition of these networks is trained to optimize an estimate of the log-likelihood, called the evidence lower bound

$$\mathcal{L}(\theta, \phi; \mathbf{x}) = \mathcal{L}_{KL}(\theta, \phi; \mathbf{x}) + \mathcal{L}_{rec}(\theta, \phi; \mathbf{x}),$$

where $\mathcal{L}_{KL}$ is the KL divergence between the approximate posterior and the prior, and $\mathcal{L}_{rec}$ is the reconstruction loss:

$$\mathcal{L}_{KL}(\theta, \phi; \mathbf{x}) = -D_{KL}(q_\phi(\mathbf{z}|\mathbf{x})||p_\theta(\mathbf{z}))$$
$$\mathcal{L}_{rec}(\theta, \phi; \mathbf{x}) = \mathbb{E}_{q_\phi(\mathbf{z}|\mathbf{x})}[\log p_\theta(\mathbf{x}|\mathbf{z})].$$

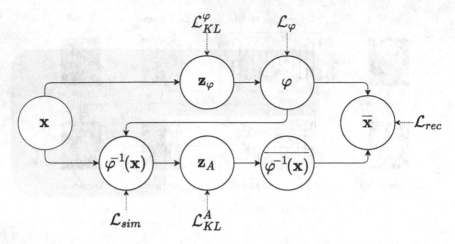

Fig. 3. Graphical model of Detlefsen and Hauberg's Conditional Variationally Inferred Transformational Autoencoder [3], with the probabilistic spatial transformer shaded in gray. By learning to sample spatial transformation parameters φ for each input $\mathbf{x}$, the model produces a disentangled latent representation $(\mathbf{z}_\varphi, \mathbf{z}_A)$ of perspective and appearance, respectively. Our implementation incorporates new loss terms $\mathcal{L}_\varphi$ and $\mathcal{L}_{sim}$ to encourage the probabilistic spatial transformer to register its inputs to a template image.

Autoencoding Appearance and Perspective. Though the standard variational autoencoder framework can learn factors of variation in a data set without supervision, it fails to include the inductive biases that are necessary for learning disentangled representations [10]. To perform unsupervised learning of representations that explicitly disentangle spatial variation, one must use a model architecture with a latent space structure that is designed for this purpose. Specifically, the latent representation should separate spatial variations (or *perspectives*) of the data from a single representation of the *appearance* of the data. In this work, we adopt the Conditional Variationally Inferred Transformational Autoencoder (VITAE) in [3] to disentangle spatial variation.

Figure 3 shows a graphical model of the VITAE framework. Each input $\mathbf{x}$ passes through a deformation network which randomly outputs a spatial transformation φ. The inverse of the spatial transformation is applied to the input to produce a conditional input $\varphi^{-1}(\mathbf{x})$ which is then reconstructed by a second encoder-decoder model. The reconstruction $\overline{\varphi^{-1}(\mathbf{x})}$ of a conditional input is then spatially transformed by φ to obtain a reconstruction $\overline{\mathbf{x}}$ of the original input. The latent variable model is thus

$$p_\theta(\mathbf{z}_\varphi, \mathbf{z}_A, \mathbf{x}) = p_\theta(\mathbf{z}_\varphi)p_\theta(\mathbf{z}_A|\mathbf{z}_\varphi)p_\theta(\mathbf{x}|\mathbf{z}_\varphi, \mathbf{z}_A),$$

where $\mathbf{z}_\varphi$ denotes an encoded perspective, $\mathbf{z}_A$ denotes an encoded appearance, and the prior $p_\theta(\mathbf{z}_\varphi, \mathbf{z}_A)$ factors into an unconditional distribution on perspectives and a conditional distribution on appearances.

Crucially, for a fixed input $\mathbf{x}$, the approximate posterior

$$q_\phi(\mathbf{z}_\varphi, \mathbf{z}_A | \mathbf{x}) = q_\phi(\mathbf{z}_\varphi | \mathbf{x}) q_\phi(\mathbf{z}_A | \mathbf{z}_\varphi, \mathbf{x})$$

factors as a product of two latent space distributions: one on encoded perspectives conditioned on the input and the other on encoded appearances conditioned on the input and the encoded perspective. Sampling from $q_\phi(\mathbf{z}_\varphi | \mathbf{x})$ and decoding the sample produces a random deformation φ which can be used to spatially transform $\mathbf{x}$.

Our main insight is to treat the VITAE framework's probabilistic spatial transformer as a variational registration model. To this end, we incorporated additional regularization terms to encourage groupwise registration: an L2 loss $\mathcal{L}_\varphi$ on the size of the spatial transformation, and a pairwise L2 loss $\mathcal{L}_{sim}$ on batches of network inputs. In particular, given a batch of inputs $\mathbf{X} = \{\mathbf{x}_i\}_{i=1}^N$, we define $\mathcal{L}_{sim}$ to be an average of L2 losses over all distinct pairs of batch elements:

$$\mathcal{L}_{sim}(\phi; \mathbf{X}) = \frac{2}{N(N-1)} \sum_{i<j} \|\varphi_i^{-1}(\mathbf{x}_i) - \varphi_j^{-1}(\mathbf{x}_j)\|, \tag{1}$$

where φ_i is the transformation associated to the instance $\mathbf{x}_i$. Furthermore, we append layers similar to those in [21] to impose explicit constraints on the size and smoothness of φ. In particular, we enforce small deformations with a hyperbolic tangent activation at the end of the perspective decoder, and we impose smoothness upon spatial transformations by convolving ϕ three times with a Gaussian kernel. The objective for this model is

$$\mathcal{L}(\theta, \phi; \mathbf{X}) = \widetilde{\mathcal{L}}(\theta, \phi; \mathbf{X}) + \mathcal{L}_\varphi(\phi; \mathbf{X}) + \mathcal{L}_{sim}(\phi; \mathbf{X}). \tag{2}$$

where, $\widetilde{\mathcal{L}} = \mathcal{L}_{KL}^\varphi + \mathcal{L}_{KL}^A + \mathcal{L}_{rec}$ is the VITAE loss.

3 Experiments

3.1 Data

The training set of the White Matter Hyperintensities Segmentation Challenge (WMH) is a data set of 60 total patients from three distinct sites: UMC Utrecht, NUHS Singapore, and VU Amsterdam [8]. Each patient has two MRIs: a T1-weighted image and a Fluid Attenuated Inversion Recovery (FLAIR) image. All MRIs are bias-field corrected, and for each patient, the T1-weighted MRI is registered to its corresponding FLAIR image. An expert observer produced segmentation maps, which were reviewed and corrected by a second expert observer. The segmentations have three labels: 0 for normal tissue, 1 for white matter hyperintensity, and 2 for other pathologies.

We further preprocessed WMH by cropping all images to the smallest volume containing non-negative voxel intensities and then padding all images to size $160 \times 192 \times 64$. Both the T1 and FLAIR modalities were stacked into a single image volume. The WMH data were then partitioned into a 40/10/10 train/validation/test split.

Input   Conditional Input   Perspective   Appearance

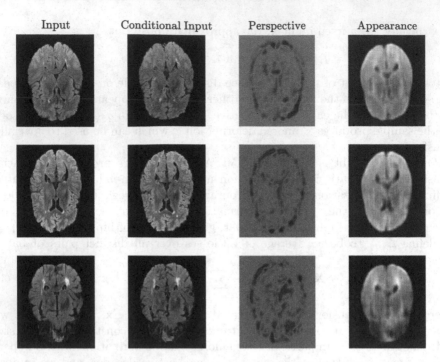

Fig. 4. Tensors produced by the VITAE model. The conditional inputs are spatial transformations of the VITAE model inputs. The VITAE framework learns to disentangle the input into a representation of the input's appearance and a spatial transformation (perspective) of the appearance.

3.2   Training Details

The segmentation network is a 3D U-Net [14] with instance normalization. Both the U-Net and VITAE architectures were implemented in TensorFlow 2.5, and the experiments were conducted with a single 40GB Nvidia A100 Tensor Core GPU. The VITAE and U-Net were trained on full-volume images for 1000 epochs with a batch size of 8 and Adam as the optimizer. For each of several different augmentation schemes (described in the next section), five U-Net replicates were trained to minimize the sum $\mathcal{L}_S$ of categorical cross-entropy and generalized Dice loss [18].

The VITAE model was trained with a constant learning rate of 1e-4. The U-Net models were trained using a polynomial learning rate schedule with an initial learning rate of 1e-4 [5]. To augment the U-Net with transformations produced from the VITAE framework, we froze the weights of the probabilistic spatial transformer and used it as an augmentation layer. Figure 2 depicts the training pipeline.

3.3 Augmentation Schemes

The U-Net architecture is exposed to a variety of data augmentation schemes. All augmentation schemes include those from a *Baseline* intensity augmentation setup closely resembling [5] and consisting of gamma correction with probability 0.3, contrast enhancement with probability 0.3, brightness transformations with probability 0.3, and Gaussian blurring with probability 0.2.

We make observations with two spatial augmentation approaches: an *Elastic* augmentation scheme which warps training volumes using elastic deformation fields constructed from random Gaussian kernels, and a *VAE* augmentation scheme which deforms training volumes using free-form deformation fields constructed from a VITAE model. Both spatial augmentations were applied with probability 0.3. Since the WMH data belongs to the low-data regime, we further extended the training set by adopting *MixUp* augmentation [22] with probability 0.3 as a third approach and combined it with elastic and VAE augmentation.

Table 1. Dice and scores of U-Net segmentation models trained on the WMH test set with different augmentation methods.

Augmentation method	Dice
Baseline	0.665 ± 0.021
Baseline+Elastic	0.671 ± 0.015
Baseline+VAE	0.671 ± 0.013
Baseline+MixUp	0.680 ± 0.008
Baseline+Elastic+MixUp	0.670 ± 0.006
Baseline+VAE+MixUp	$\mathbf{0.684 \pm 0.011}$

3.4 Results and Discussion

We use the Dice score to evaluate the performance of U-Nets trained to segment white matter hyperintensities. Table 1 shows our results. The scheme combining VITAE augmentation and MixUp augmentation yielded the highest mean Dice score, nearly a 2% improvement over the baseline augmentation setup. A one-sided unequal-variances t-test comparing this augmentation scheme against the baseline indicated statistical significance at the 8.3% level. This suggests that a combination of data-independent mixture augmentation and data-driven spatial augmentation could improve the performance of a deep segmentation model, particularly on data sets featuring high variation among abnormality shapes. Further investigation of this method with additional data sets and more extensive validation is needed.

4   Conclusion

We proposed a framework for performing instance-specific data augmentation via unsupervised spatial disentanglement. The proposed method expands a training set by spatially transforming inputs using sampled deformations from a data-dependent distribution. Preliminary experimental results on the White Matter Hyperintensities Challenge 2017 data set suggest that this method in combination with MixUp augmentation can improve the performance of a segmentation network and compares favorably with other methods of spatial data augmentation.

Acknowledgement. This work is supported by Innovation Fund Denmark.

References

1. Balakrishnan, G., Zhao, A., Sabuncu, M.R., Guttag, J., Dalca, A.V.: Voxel-Morph: a learning framework for deformable medical image registration. IEEE Trans. Med. Imaging **38**(8), 1788–1800 (2019). https://doi.org/10.1109/TMI.2019.2897538. https://ieeexplore.ieee.org/document/8633930/
2. Bepler, T., Zhong, E.D., Kelley, K., Brignole, E., Berger, B.: Explicitly disentangling image content from translation and rotation with spatial-VAE. In: Advances in Neural Information Processing Systems, pp. 15409–15419 (2019). http://arxiv.org/abs/1909.11663
3. Detlefsen, N.S., Hauberg, S.: Explicit disentanglement of appearance and perspective in generative models. In: Advances in Neural Information Processing Systems, pp. 1016–1026 (2019). http://arxiv.org/abs/1906.11881
4. Hauberg, S., Freifeld, O., Lindbo Larsen, A.B., Fisher, J.W., Hansen, L.K.: Dreaming more data: class-dependent distributions over diffeomorphisms for learned data augmentation. In: Proceedings of 19th International Conference on Artificial Intelligence and Statistics, pp. 342–350 (2016)
5. Isensee, F., Jaeger, P.F., Kohl, S.A.A., Petersen, J., Maier-Hein, K.H.: nnU-Net: a self-configuring method for deep learning-based biomedical image segmentation. Nat. Methods **18**(2), 203–211 (2021). https://doi.org/10.1038/s41592-020-01008-z. https://doi.org/10.1038/s41592-020-01008-zhttp://www.nature.com/articles/s41592-020-01008-z
6. Jaderberg, M., Simonyan, K., Zisserman, A., Kavukcuoglu, K.: Spatial transformer networks. In: Advances in Neural Information Processing Systems, 2015-January, pp. 2017–2025 (2015)
7. Kingma, D.P., Welling, M.: Auto-encoding variational bayes. In: 2nd International Conference on Learning Representations, ICLR 2014 - Conference Track Proceedings (ML), pp. 1–14 (2014)
8. Kuijf, H.J., et al.: Standardized assessment of automatic segmentation of white matter hyperintensities and results of the WMH segmentation challenge. IEEE Trans. Med. Imaging **38**(11), 2556–2568 (2019). https://doi.org/10.1109/TMI.2019.2905770
9. Locatello, F., et al.: A commentary on the unsupervised learning of disentangled representations. In: AAAI 2020–34th AAAI Conference on Artificial Intelligence, pp. 13681–13684 (2020). https://doi.org/10.1609/aaai.v34i09.7120. http://arxiv.org/abs/2007.14184

10. Locatello, F., et al.: Challenging common assumptions in the unsupervised learning of disentangled representations. In: 36th International Conference on Machine Learning, ICML 2019, pp. 7247–7283 (2019)
11. Olut, S., Shen, Z., Xu, Z., Gerber, S., Niethammer, M.: Adversarial data augmentation via deformation statistics. In: Vedaldi, A., Bischof, H., Brox, T., Frahm, J.-M. (eds.) ECCV 2020. LNCS, vol. 12374, pp. 643–659. Springer, Cham (2020). https://doi.org/10.1007/978-3-030-58526-6_38
12. Orbes, M., et al.: PADDIT: probabilistic augmentation of data using diffeomorphic image transformation. In: Angelini, E.D., Landman, B.A. (eds.) Medical Imaging 2019 Image Processing, vol. 10949, p. 27. SPIE (2019). https://doi.org/10.1117/12.2512520
13. Qin, C., Shi, B., Liao, R., Mansi, T., Rueckert, D., Kamen, A.: Unsupervised deformable registration for multi-modal images via disentangled representations. In: Chung, A.C.S., Gee, J.C., Yushkevich, P.A., Bao, S. (eds.) IPMI 2019. LNCS, vol. 11492, pp. 249–261. Springer, Cham (2019). https://doi.org/10.1007/978-3-030-20351-1_19
14. Ronneberger, O., Fischer, P., Brox, T.: U-Net: convolutional networks for biomedical image segmentation. In: Navab, N., Hornegger, J., Wells, W.M., Frangi, A.F. (eds.) MICCAI 2015. LNCS, vol. 9351, pp. 234–241. Springer, Cham (2015). https://doi.org/10.1007/978-3-319-24574-4_28
15. Schwöbel, P., Warburg, F., Jørgensen, M., Madsen, K.H., Hauberg, S.: Probabilistic Spatial Transformer Networks. arXiv (2020). http://arxiv.org/abs/2004.03637
16. Shorten, C., Khoshgoftaar, T.M.: A survey on image data augmentation for deep learning. J. Big Data 6(1), 1–48 (2019). https://doi.org/10.1186/s40537-019-0197-0
17. Shu, Z., Sahasrabudhe, M., Alp Güler, R., Samaras, D., Paragios, N., Kokkinos, I.: Deforming autoencoders: unsupervised disentangling of shape and appearance. In: Ferrari, V., Hebert, M., Sminchisescu, C., Weiss, Y. (eds.) ECCV 2018. LNCS, vol. 11214, pp. 664–680. Springer, Cham (2018). https://doi.org/10.1007/978-3-030-01249-6_40
18. Sudre, C.H., Li, W., Vercauteren, T., Ourselin, S., Jorge Cardoso, M.: Generalised dice overlap as a deep learning loss function for highly unbalanced segmentations. In: Cardoso, M.J., et al. (eds.) DLMIA/ML-CDS -2017. LNCS, vol. 10553, pp. 240–248. Springer, Cham (2017). https://doi.org/10.1007/978-3-319-67558-9_28
19. Tang, Z., Chen, K., Pan, M., Wang, M., Song, Z.: An augmentation strategy for medical image processing based on statistical shape model and 3D thin plate spline for deep learning. IEEE Access 7, 133111–133121 (2019). https://doi.org/10.1109/ACCESS.2019.2941154
20. Uzunova, H., Handels, H., Ehrhardt, J.: Guided filter regularization for improved disentanglement of shape and appearance in diffeomorphic autoencoders. In: Proceedings of Fourth Conference on Medical Imaging with Deep Learning, pp. 774–786. PMLR (2021). https://proceedings.mlr.press/v143/uzunova21a.html%7D
21. Wyburd, M.K., Dinsdale, N.K., Namburete, A.I.L., Jenkinson, M.: TEDS-Net: enforcing diffeomorphisms in spatial transformers to guarantee topology preservation in segmentations. In: de Bruijne, M., et al. (eds.) MICCAI 2021. LNCS, vol. 12901, pp. 250–260. Springer, Cham (2021). https://doi.org/10.1007/978-3-030-87193-2_24

22. Zhang, H., Cisse, M., Dauphin, Y.N., Lopez-Paz, D.: MixUp: beyond empirical risk minimization. In: 6th International Conference on Learning Representations, ICLR 2018 - Conference Track Proceedings, pp. 1–13 (2018)
23. Zhao, A., Balakrishnan, G., Durand, F., Guttag, J.V., Dalca, A.V.: Data augmentation using learned transformations for one-shot medical image segmentation. In: 2019 IEEE/CVF Conference on Computer Vision and Pattern Recognition, pp. 8535–8545. IEEE (2019). https://doi.org/10.1109/CVPR.2019.00874. https://ieeexplore.ieee.org/document/8953991/

Low-Rank and Sparse Metamorphic Autoencoders for Unsupervised Pathology Disentanglement

Hristina Uzunova[1], Heinz Handels[1,2], and Jan Ehrhardt[1,2(✉)]

[1] German Research Center for Artificial Intelligence, Lübeck, Germany
[2] Institute of Medical Informatics, University of Lübeck, Lübeck, Germany
jan.ehrhardt@uni-luebeck.de

Abstract. In order to establish population-based analysis of image data from multi-center studies, it is often helpful to disentangle images in their shape and appearance components. However, abnormal (e.g. pathological) and normal appearances of images strongly differ and should ideally be separated in the modeling process. In this work, we propose a metamorphic autoencoder for the disentanglement of shape as well as normal and abnormal appearance of medical images by integrating a low-rank and sparse decomposition into the training process. Experiments show that this method can reliably be used for unsupervised pathology disentanglement opening perspectives for unsupervised pathology segmentation, pseudo-healthy image synthesis and conditional image generation.

Keywords: Low-rank and sparse · Metamorphic autoencoders · Unsupervised anomaly detection

1 Introduction

The disentanglement of shape and appearance is a common computer vision task [6,15,26] and has become more and more prominent for the medical image domain in the past few years [13,23]. Typically, medical images within a dataset would be acquired in different hospitals, using different devices or parameter settings. Thus, in order to establish population-based analysis, it is important to distinguish between the anatomical shape variations and the differing (device-dependent) intensity profiles. The precursor of deep-learning based disentanglement approaches are statistical shape and appearance models, with separate representations for both [23], however, they require tedious data preprocessing, e.g. for landmark extraction. Thus, deep learning based disentanglement has gained on popularity in the recent years. Most frequently, approaches based on variational autoencoders [9], generative adversarial networks [10] and normalizing flows [12] are used. For the disentanglement of shape and appearance in particular, approaches based on the metamorphic template paradigm are a common choice. They assume that images can be represented as deformed versions of a given template. For example, diffeomorphic autoencoders [2] model images as spatial displacement offsets to a dynamically generated template, however, do not consider

J. Fragemann et al. (Eds.): MAD 2022, LNCS 13823, pp. 59–69, 2023.
https://doi.org/10.1007/978-3-031-25046-0_6

any occurring appearance changes. A similar approach from [19] generates an appearance template and a displacement field for each given image. Yet, a major drawback of this method is the lack of a global template for the given dataset and the limited disentanglement reliability due to the implicit shape and appearance modeling. To cope with those problems, [22] proposes an approach for the simultaneous shape and appearance modeling as spatial and intensity offsets to a global template, by introducing a Guided Filter [8] based regularization to the appearance map in order to improve the disentanglement between the two components.

These works concentrate on images of normal anatomical appearances, however, the problem of disentanglement becomes even more complex, when the images contain pathological or other abnormal structures, since they distort the normal anatomy. Therefore, another frequent disentanglement task is the so-called disease decomposition, or the disentanglement of normal and abnormal features in the images. The most common approach is pseudo-healthy synthesis, e.g. [25], where generative adversarial networks are used to generate the healthy equivalent of pathological images, thus, the pathological structures can be represented as the difference between the original image and its pseudo-healthy reconstruction. The authors of [11], present another approach for the normal/abnormal disentanglement by using a codebook-based approach directly in the latent space and restricting the latent space of pathological structures by solving an auxiliary segmentation task. Such methods, are, however, supervised and need the ground truth pathology segmentation in order to establish the disentanglement. Furthermore, they rely on a relatively coherent training dataset. In [5], the authors propose a generative variational autoencoder in order to distinguish between time-dependent disease changes in brain MRIs and inter-patient variability. However, this approach requires high-quality longitudinal data which are rarely available.

A more classical approach for the disentanglement of normal and abnormal structures is the low-rank and sparse decomposition of images, originally used for the robust alignment of natural images containing some sparse errors [17] and later applied for medical image registration of pathological data [14,21]. The idea of our work is to integrate this disentanglement approach in a neural network architecture which has been successfully shown, e.g. in [18], where the authors establish an unsupervised segmentation by training a U-Net for separating sparse from low-rank components.In this work, we integrate the low-rank and sparse decomposition approach in the autoencoder architecture from [22] and establish an unsupervised approach for the population-based disentanglement of shape, normal and abnormal appearance in medical images.

2   Methods

2.1   Guided Filter Regularized Metamorphic Autoencoder

Deformable autoencoders aim to disentangle shape and appearance information by reconstructing input images X as compositions of a deformation-free appearance template image T and a deformation field φ such that $X \approx T \circ \varphi$

with $\circ$ denoting the warping of the template with the displacement field. Some approaches consider either a separate template for each image [19] or a global appearance template for all images [2]. The former approaches do not allow population-based analysis, and the quality of the disentanglement is mainly driven by the capacity of the latent shape and appearance encodings. The latter approaches model only spatial deformations of the template and neglect individual appearance deviations. Hence, [3,22] propose to consider the image-specific appearance Δ_{A_i} and shape φ_i for each image X_i using a universal global template image T such that $X_i \approx (T + \Delta_{A_i}) \circ \varphi_i$. Here, φ_i is a displacement field, that maps the template to the image space and Δ_{A_i} approximates the pixel-wise intensity difference $(T - X_i \circ \varphi_i^{-1})$. We also refer to Δ_{A_i} as "appearance map".

However, Δ_{A_i} and φ_i compete with each other because differences to the template can be reduced by both local deformations and local intensity changes, making it difficult to disentangle the two components. Therefore, [22] introduces a Guided Filter [8] regularization of the appearance map so that it cannot change the shape of anatomical structures, but can only adjust the intensity of structures already included in the template. The Guided Filter is integrated into the network as the last layer of the appearance decoder in a fully differentiable manner as proposed by [24]. It takes in the current global template as guidance and smooths the predicted appearance map according to it. Thus, the shape of the structures given by the template cannot be altered and no new structures can be inserted by the appearance map.

The final training objective is a composite of a reconstruction loss $\mathcal{L}_{rec}$, a regularization for the displacement field $\mathcal{L}_{reg}$ and the Kullback-Leibler regularization of the latent space $\mathcal{L}_{KL}$ [22]:

$$\mathcal{L} = \alpha \mathcal{L}_{rec}\big(X, (T + \Delta_A) \circ \varphi\big) + \mathcal{L}_{KL}\big(\mathcal{N}(0,1), \mathcal{N}(\mu_z, \sigma_z)\big) + \mathcal{L}_{reg}(\varphi), \qquad (1)$$

with $\mathcal{L}_{rec}$ being an MSE loss and the regularizer $\mathcal{L}_{reg}(\varphi) = \gamma \sum_j^d \|\nabla v^{(j)}\|_2^2 + \xi \|v\|_1$ is a composite of a diffusion and an $\mathcal{L}^1$ regularization of the velocity field v resulting from φ. The image dimension is denoted d, and α, γ, ξ are weighting parameters.

The purely metamorphic approach in [3] does not account for normal intensity variations in the images, e.g., scanner-related differences or multimodal data, and assumes that only pathologies are represented in the appearance map, whereas the guided filtering approach [22] has been shown to provide better disentanglement of shape and appearance, especially for multimodal data, but cannot be used to model pathological structures since they strongly vary from the computed template. For this reason, this work considers an additional pathological appearance component Δ_P that can be generated independently from normal anatomical appearance variations such that an input image X_i can now be reconsidered as $X_i \approx (T + \Delta_{A_i} + \Delta_{P_i}) \circ \varphi_i$.

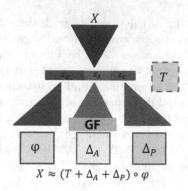

$$X \approx (T + \Delta_A + \Delta_P) \circ \varphi$$

Fig. 1. Schematic representation of the proposed autoencoder and the reconstruction objective. Colors correspond to encoder ■, shape decoder ■, anatomical appearance decoder ■, pathology decoder ■ and implicitly generated parameterized template ■. (Color figure online)

2.2   Low-Rank and Sparse Image Decomposition for Normal/ Abnormal Disentanglement

Given a population of n images of the same body region, the goal of this work is an unsupervised learning of a disentanglement in three components: Shape and intensity variations with respect to a (learned) template, as well as pathological structures. All three components are generated by an autoencoder architecture with three separate decoders, where the encoder generates a composite latent vector $z = [z_\varphi, z_A, z_P]$ and each part of it is used respectively as an input to the shape, appearance and pathology decoders. The template is implicitly generated through backpropagation (Fig. 1).

An objective based on the similarity of the input image with its reconstruction according to Eq. (1) will not provide sufficient disentanglement of the separate representations of pathology and anatomy since the network can freely map the components z_A and z_P to image features. For this reason, we propose a low-rank and sparse decomposition approach to facilitate normal and abnormal disentanglement. Using a low-rank and sparse decomposition for pathology disentanglement is based on the assumption that aligned images of the healthy anatomy of the same image domain are highly correlated, thus, a low-rank representation can be established between them. Hence, structures not fitting this representation can be separated in a sparse error component. Many pathological structures such as lesions and tumors, observed in our experiments, can then be assumed to be contained in this sparse component as their presence disrupts the low-rank representation. However, there is a number of abnormalities such as Alzheimer's disease that do not comply with this assumption and need to be considered separately.

Let $D = [d^{(1)}, ..., d^{(n)}] \in \mathbb{R}^{m \times n}$ be a sequence of m-dimensional vectorized data representations. We model $D = A + E$ as a decomposition into the sequences $A \in \mathbb{R}^{m \times n}$ and $E \in \mathbb{R}^{m \times n}$ corresponding respectively to the normal image anatomy and individual deviations such as abnormalities or pathological structures. Further, when the images in D are aligned, i.e. registered, the image normal anatomy is highly correlated between individuals and, thus, we assume A has a *low-rank* structure. Pathologies are not consistent with this low-rank structure and represented in a *sparse* error term E.

Hence, this approach is called low-rank and sparse image decomposition (L&S) and can be represented as the optimization problem:

$$\min_{A,E} \operatorname{rank}(A) + \lambda ||E||_0, \text{ s.t. } D = A + E$$

with weight $\lambda > 0$. While this optimization problem naturally follows from the problem definition, it is not directly tractable. Thus a relaxed convex optimization is used instead replacing the rank function and $\mathcal{L}^0$ norm with the nuclear norm $|| \cdot ||_\star$ and $\mathcal{L}^1$ norm. Given a sequence of input images $(X_i)_{i=1,\dots,n}$ with the matrix representation $\tilde{X} = [vec(X_1)| \dots |vec(X_n)] \in \mathbb{R}^{m \times n}$ and $\tilde{\Delta}_A, \tilde{\Delta}_P$ the corresponding representations of appearance map and pathologies, the low-rank and sparse optimization problem is formulated as:

$$\mathcal{L}_{LS}(T, \Delta_A, \Delta_P) = ||\tilde{T} + \tilde{\Delta}_A||_\star + \lambda ||\tilde{\Delta}_P||_1 \to \min_{T, \Delta_A, \Delta_P},$$
$$\text{s.t. } \tilde{X} \circ \varphi^{-1} = \tilde{T} + \tilde{\Delta}_A + \tilde{\Delta}_P \tag{2}$$

where $\tilde{X} \circ \varphi^{-1} = [vec(X_1 \circ \varphi_1^{-1})| \dots |vec(X_n \circ \varphi_n^{-1})]$ represents the images transformed into the template space, and $\tilde{T}$ is the n-fold replicated template.

To integrate Eq. (2) into the network training, we evaluate $\mathcal{L}_{LS}$ for batches of size n, and during the backpropagation we use a proximal mapping to compute gradients of Eq. (2) at the current estimate $\mathbf{x}^t$, since $\mathbf{x}^t - \operatorname{prox}_{\mathcal{L}_{LS}}(\mathbf{x}^t) \in \partial \mathcal{L}_{LS}$.[1] For solving the proximal operator $\operatorname{prox}_{\mathcal{L}_{LS}}(\mathbf{x}) = \arg\min_{\mathbf{u}} \mathcal{L}_{LS}(\mathbf{u}) + \frac{1}{2}||\mathbf{u} - \mathbf{x}||_2^2$ iterative forward-backward splitting is applied [4], however other methods as alternating directions [17] can be used as well.

We propose to integrate the low-rank and sparse decomposition of $\tilde{\Delta}_A$ and $\tilde{\Delta}_P$ into the training objective from Eq. (1) as follows:

$$\mathcal{L} = \alpha \mathcal{L}_{rec}(X, (T + \Delta_A + \Delta_P) \circ \varphi) + \beta \mathcal{L}_{LS}(T, \Delta_A, \Delta_P)$$
$$+ \mathcal{L}_{KL}(\mathcal{N}(0,1), \mathcal{N}(\mu_z, \sigma_z)) + \mathcal{L}_{reg}(\varphi), \tag{3}$$

with weights α and β to balance the similarity based reconstruction loss and the L&S decomposition.

Using this approach, pathological structures are expected to be contained within the sparse component E due to their disturbance of the low-rank structure of A. Thus, a disease disentanglement is established in a completely unsupervised manner without using any prior knowledge such as pathology segmentations.

---

[1] To simplify notation, we use $\mathbf{x}$ (or $\mathbf{u}$) instead of $(\tilde{T}, \tilde{\Delta}_A, \tilde{\Delta}_P)$ in this paragraph.

3   Experiments and Results

Data: For the following experiments a composite dataset containing brain MRIs of healthy controls and brain tumor patients is used. The collected healthy images are 581 t1 MRIs from the IXI dataset[2] and the pathological images feature 369 t1c tumor MRIs from the BraTS 2020 dataset [16]. The ground truth tumor segmentations of the BraTS data are only used for evaluation purposes here. All images are skull-stripped, affinely pre-registered and the 75th axial slice of each image is extracted. The data is used in a 80/20 train/test split.

Implementation Details: For the final objective, the regularization weighting parameters γ and ξ are set to 10 chosen in accordance to [22]. For the L&S loss, an L&S solver predicts Δ_A and Δ_P for 10 iterations for each batch of warped images. The loss weighting parameters α and β are chosen to be 10 and 20, respectively. The parameter λ is chosen analogously to [17].

The proposed architecture contains an encoder with three convolutional layers with stride two and two fully connected layers for the mapping to the mean and standard deviation vectors respectively. The decoder contains a fully-connected layer mapping the latent vector to the feature space and three convolutional layers combined with a bilinear upsampling layer that doubles the image size before each convolution. We use tangens hyperbolicus activation functions between all layers. The encoder and decoder use the mirroring channels numbers $[32, 64, 128]$ and vice versa. In our experience, the sizes z_A and z_P can be set to 64, where as z_φ requires more dimensions (here: 256). The network is trained for 1000 epochs, however, an early stopping strategy is used if the loss does not improve over the span of 50 epochs. Further, the batch size is set to 50 and an Adam optimizer with a learning rate of $1e^{-4}$ is used.

Reconstruction Ability: In the first experiment, the reconstruction ability of the proposed method is evaluated. Here, the difference between the real test images and their reconstructions using the proposed approach is calculated using mean squared error (MSE), mean absolute error (MAE) and structured similarity index (SSIM) (Table 1). It can be observed that for the different subsets – healthy and pathological – similar results are achieved, which indicates that the pathological variability is well represented. Overall, good reconstruction can be observed with results comparable to [22] that achieves an SSIM of 0.87 on T1 MRI brain dataset of healthy subjects.

Pathology Disentanglement: To evaluate how well the pathological structures are disentangled from the normal anatomy, a qualitative analysis is proposed in the first step. Figure 2 shows two pathological and one healthy images and their deduced pathology and healthy appearance components. It quickly becomes obvious that the pathology map of the BraTS images contains mostly the tumors themselves. This is also confirmed by the reconstruction of the pseudo-healthy images, where not adding the pathology map leads to a missing

---

[2] www.brain-development.org.

Table 1. Reconstruction ability of the proposed approach for the healthy and pathological subsets, as well as the combined dataset. Note that the scaling of the images in a [0,1] range affects the used metrics.

Dataset	MSE ↓	MAE↓	SSIM ↑
	Mean ± Std	Mean ± Std	Mean ± Std
Healthy	0.003 ± 0.001	0.028 ± 0.005	0.848 ± 0.025
Pathological	0.004 ± 0.001	0.026 ± 0.005	0.840 ± 0.034
All	0.003 ± 0.001	0.028 ± 0.005	0.845 ± 0.031

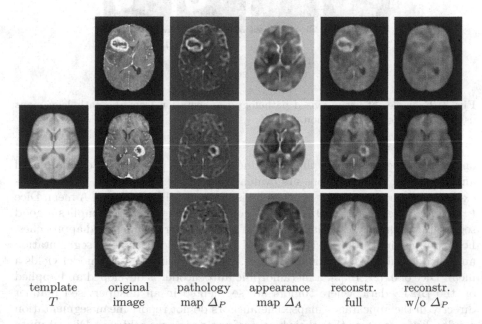

| template T | original image | pathology map Δ_P | appearance map Δ_A | reconstr. full | reconstr. w/o Δ_P |

Fig. 2. Qualitative analysis of the pathology disentanglement. First two rows T1c MRIs from BraTS; last row T1 MRI from IXI. Note that for visualization purposes the pathology/appearance maps are scaled in [0,1].

pathological structure but no further significant changes in the image appearance. Due to the nature of the L&S method, however, the pathology map also contains further small image details, e.g. for the BraTS images, non-tumorous contrasting tissue is also included in Δ_P. This also leads to the pathology map not only containing zero values for healthy images, yet, it does not include any significant anatomical structures, which can be concluded based on the similarity of the full reconstruction and the reconstruction without Δ_P (note that for visualization purposes the pathology/appearance maps are scaled in [0,1], thus, low values might appear high).

To quantify the pathology disentanglement, a further pathology segmentation experiment is proposed, where the Chan-Vese segmentation [7] approach is used

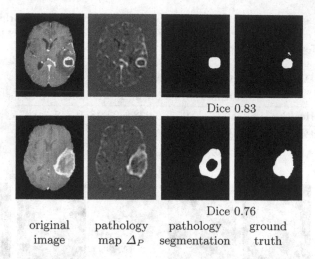

Dice 0.83

Dice 0.76

original   pathology   pathology   ground
image   map Δ_P segmentation   truth

Fig. 3. Examples of unsupervised pathology segmentation from the pathology maps using a Chan-Vese segmentation.

on the pathology maps. For this experiment, only the pathological data are used and the tumor segmentations are evaluated over the union of all tumor labels excluding the edema since it is not well visible in t1 MRI sequences. A mean Dice ($\pm$ standard deviation) of **0.75 $\pm$ 0.14** could be achieved, which implies a good segmentation quality, especially in comparison to other unsupervised approaches. For example in [1], out of 17 compared unsupervised pathology segmentation autoencoder models on a glioma dataset, the best resulting VAE-model yields a mean Dice of 0.522. In [3], a metamorphic autoencoder is developed and applied on the BraTS data, where tumors are segmented in an unsupervised manner directly in the appearance maps. The authors do not report mean segmentation results, however, state that their best performing images achieve a Dice of up to 0.7. The good segmentation ability of our approach indicates that the pathology maps mostly feature pathological structures, thus, a good disentanglement can be achieved (see Fig. 3 for examples).

4   Discussion and Conclusion

In this work, we presented an unsupervised approach for the disentanglement of medical images into shape variations, as well as anatomical (healthy) and pathological appearance using a metamorphic autoencoder. Guided filtering is employed to facilitate the disentanglement of shape and appearance, whereas to disentangle healthy and pathological appearance, a low-rank and sparse decomposition is injected into the metamorphic autoencoder. Previous work [22] has shown that the Guided filtering leads to a robust and plausible uncoupling of shape and appearance information, however, it impedes the representation of pathological structures. The method proposed in this work overcomes this limitation and enables fully unsupervised disease disentanglement.

In first experiments, this method shows good disentanglement results, where pathological structures such as brain tumors can be represented as sparse image parts. This is underlined by the good unsupervised segmentation of the pathological structures achieved in the experiments. Even though mostly pathological structures are contained in the sparse image representations, the purely unsupervised nature of the proposed method, cannot completely prevent other small structures from being represented by the sparse image part. As our visual assessment confirms, these often include contrasting tissue from the T1c sequences or other rare structures. In order to evaluate the disentanglement more thoroughly, a more extensive experimental analysis is required comparing the proposed approach to existing methods.

A limitation of the proposed approach is the fact that only appearance-based abnormalities can be modeled, e.g. the differing intensity values of tumor tissue, however, abnormal spatial deformations of the tissue are not explicitly represented. This is disadvantageous for some pathology types like Alzheimer's disease that primarily change the shape of the anatomical structures. Also, no pathology-induced deformations can be modeled, e.g. tumor-mass effect [20]. Thus, future work will consider to disentangle not only the appearance maps, but also the deformation fields into their healthy and pathological components. Also, to enhance the practical application of the method, an adaptation for 3D medical image volumes is required.

An advantageous ability of the proposed approach, that requires further investigation in the future, is pseudo-healthy image generation qualitatively evaluated in our experiments. This can be used as a pre-step to many medical image processing tasks, e.g. image registration of images with missing correspondences. Overall, the proposed fully unsupervised disease disentanglement approach shows promising properties and opens up possibilities for various applications in the medical image processing domain.

References

1. Baur, C., Denner, S., Wiestler, B., Navab, N., Albarqouni, S.: Autoencoders for unsupervised anomaly segmentation in brain MR images: a comparative study. Med. Image Anal. **69**, 101952 (2021)
2. Bône, A., Louis, M., Colliot, O., Durrleman, S.: Learning low-dimensional representations of shape data sets with diffeomorphic autoencoders. In: Chung, A.C.S., Gee, J.C., Yushkevich, P.A., Bao, S. (eds.) IPMI 2019. LNCS, vol. 11492, pp. 195–207. Springer, Cham (2019). https://doi.org/10.1007/978-3-030-20351-1_15
3. Bône, A., Vernhet, P., Colliot, O., Durrleman, S.: Learning joint shape and appearance representations with metamorphic auto-encoders. In: Martel, A.L., et al. (eds.) MICCAI 2020. LNCS, vol. 12261, pp. 202–211. Springer, Cham (2020). https://doi.org/10.1007/978-3-030-59710-8_20
4. Combettes, P.L., Wajs, V.R.: Signal recovery by proximal forward-backward splitting. Multiscale Model. Simul. **4**(4), 1168–1200 (2005)

5. Couronné, R., Vernhet, P., Durrleman, S.: Longitudinal self-supervision to disentangle inter-patient variability from disease progression. In: de Bruijne, M., et al. (eds.) MICCAI 2021. LNCS, vol. 12902, pp. 231–241. Springer, Cham (2021). https://doi.org/10.1007/978-3-030-87196-3_22

6. Ding, Z., et al.: Guided variational autoencoder for disentanglement learning. In: 2020 IEEE/CVF Conference on Computer Vision and Pattern Recognition (CVPR), Seattle, WA, USA, pp. 7917–7926. IEEE, June 2020

7. Getreuer, P.: Chan-Vese segmentation. Image Process. On Line **2**, 214–224 (2012)

8. He, K., Sun, J., Tang, X.: Guided image filtering. IEEE Trans. Pattern Anal. Mach. Intell. **35**(6), 1397–1409 (2013)

9. Higgins, I., et al.: Beta-VAE: learning basic visual concepts with a constrained variational framework. In: International Conference on Learning Representations, July 2022

10. Kazemi, H., Iranmanesh, S.M., Nasrabadi, N.: Style and content disentanglement in generative adversarial networks. In: 2019 IEEE Winter Conference on Applications of Computer Vision (WACV), pp. 848–856, January 2019

11. Kobayashi, K., et al.: Decomposing normal and abnormal features of medical images for content-based image retrieval of glioma imaging. Med. Image Anal. **74**, 102227 (2021)

12. Kondo, R., Kawano, K., Koide, S., Kutsuna, T. :Flow-based image-to-image translation with feature disentanglement. In: Advances in Neural Information Processing Systems, vol. 32. Curran Associates Inc. (2019)

13. Liu, S., Dowling, J., Engstrom, C., Greer, P., Crozier, S., Chandra, S.: Manipulating Medical Image Translation with Manifold Disentanglement, November 2020

14. Liu, X., Niethammer, M., Kwitt, R., Singh, N., McCormick, M., Aylward, S.: Low-rank atlas image analyses in the presence of pathologies. IEEE Trans. Med. Imaging **34**(12), 2583–2591 (2015)

15. Lorenz, D., Bereska, L., Milbich, T., Ommer, B.: Unsupervised Part-Based Disentangling of Object Shape and Appearance. arXiv:1903.06946, June 2019

16. Menze, B.H., et al.: The multimodal brain tumor image segmentation benchmark (BRATS). IEEE Trans. Med. Imaging **34**(10), 1993–2024 (2015)

17. Peng, Y., Ganesh, A., Wright, J., Xu, W., Ma, Y.: RASL: robust alignment by sparse and low-rank decomposition for linearly correlated images. IEEE Trans. Pattern Anal. Mach. Intell. **34**(11), 2233–2246 (2012)

18. Sakai, T.: Unsupervised Deep Learning by Injecting Low-Rank and Sparse Priors. arXiv (2021)

19. Shu, Z., Sahasrabudhe, M., Alp Güler, R., Samaras, D., Paragios, N., Kokkinos, I.: Deforming autoencoders: unsupervised disentangling of shape and appearance. In: Ferrari, V., Hebert, M., Sminchisescu, C., Weiss, Y. (eds.) ECCV 2018. LNCS, vol. 11214, pp. 664–680. Springer, Cham (2018). https://doi.org/10.1007/978-3-030-01249-6_40

20. Uzunova, H., Ehrhardt, J., Handels, H.: Generation of annotated brain tumor MRIs with tumor-induced tissue deformations for training and assessment of neural networks. In: Martel, A.L., et al. (eds.) MICCAI 2020. LNCS, vol. 12264, pp. 501–511. Springer, Cham (2020). https://doi.org/10.1007/978-3-030-59719-1_49

21. Uzunova, H., Handels, H., Ehrhardt, J.: Robust groupwise affine registration of medical images with stochastic optimization. In: Maier-Hein, geb. Fritzsche, K., Deserno, geb. Lehmann, T., Handels, H., Tolxdorff, T. (eds.) Bildverarbeitung für die Medizin 2017. I, pp. 62–67. Springer, Heidelberg (2017). https://doi.org/10.1007/978-3-662-54345-0_20

22. Uzunova, H., Handels, H., Ehrhardt, J.: Guided filter regularization for improved disentanglement of shape and appearance in diffeomorphic autoencoders. In: Proceedings of the Fourth Conference on Medical Imaging with Deep Learning. PMLR, pp. 774–786, August 2021
23. Wilms, M., Handels, H., Ehrhardt, J.: Representative patch-based active appearance models generated from small training populations. In: Descoteaux, M., Maier-Hein, L., Franz, A., Jannin, P., Collins, D.L., Duchesne, S. (eds.) MICCAI 2017. LNCS, vol. 10433, pp. 152–160. Springer, Cham (2017). https://doi.org/10.1007/978-3-319-66182-7_18
24. Wu, H., Zheng, S., Zhang, J., Huang, K.: Fast end-to-end trainable guided filter. In: 2018 IEEE/CVF Conference on Computer Vision and Pattern Recognition (Salt Lake City, UT), pp. 1838–1847. IEEE, June 2018
25. Xia, T., Chartsias, A., Tsaftaris, S.A.: Pseudo-healthy synthesis with pathology disentanglement and adversarial learning. Med. Image Anal. **64**, 101719 (2020)
26. Yang, H., Zhang, T., Huang, W., He, X., Porikli, F.: Towards purely unsupervised disentanglement of appearance and shape for person images generation. In: Proceedings of the 1st International Workshop on Human-Centric Multimedia Analysis (Seattle WA USA), pp. 33–41. ACM, October 2020

Training β-VAE by Aggregating a Learned Gaussian Posterior with a Decoupled Decoder

Jianning Li[1,2]($\boxtimes$), Jana Fragemann[1], Seyed-Ahmad Ahmadi[3], Jens Kleesiek[1], and Jan Egger[1,2]

[1] Institute for AI in Medicine, University Medicine Essen, Essen, Germany
Jianning.Li@uk-essen.de
[2] Institute of Computer Graphics and Vision, Graz University of Technology, Graz, Austria
[3] NVIDIA, Munich, Germany

Abstract. The reconstruction loss and the Kullback-Leibler divergence (KLD) loss in a variational autoencoder (VAE) often play antagonistic roles, and tuning the weight of the KLD loss in β-VAE to achieve a balance between the two losses is a tricky and dataset-specific task. As a result, current practices in VAE training often result in a trade-off between the reconstruction fidelity and the continuity/disentanglement of the latent space, if the weight β is not carefully tuned. In this paper, we present intuitions and a careful analysis of the antagonistic mechanism of the two losses, and propose, based on the insights, a simple yet effective two-stage method for training a VAE. Specifically, the method aggregates a learned Gaussian posterior $z \sim q_\theta(z|x)$ with a decoder decoupled from the KLD loss, which is trained to learn a new conditional distribution $p_\phi(x|z)$ of the input data x. Experimentally, we show that the aggregated VAE maximally satisfies the Gaussian assumption about the latent space, while still achieves a reconstruction error comparable to when the latent space is only loosely regularized by $\mathcal{N}(\mathbf{0}, I)$. The proposed approach does not require hyperparameter (i.e., the KLD weight β) tuning given a specific dataset as required in common VAE training practices. We evaluate the method using a medical dataset intended for 3D skull reconstruction and shape completion, and the results indicate promising generative capabilities of the VAE trained using the proposed method. Besides, through guided manipulation of the latent variables, we establish a connection between existing autoencoder (AE)-based approaches and generative approaches, such as VAE, for the shape completion problem. Codes and pre-trained weights are available at https://github.com/Jianningli/skullVAE.

Keywords: VAE · Disentanglement · Latent representation · Skull reconstruction · Shape completion

This work was supported by the REACT-EU project KITE (Plattform für KI-Translation Essen).

J. Fragemann et al. (Eds.): MAD 2022, LNCS 13823, pp. 70–92, 2023.
https://doi.org/10.1007/978-3-031-25046-0_7

1   Introduction

Researches on autoencoder (AE)-based generative frameworks such as variational autoencoder (VAE) [19], β-VAE [14] and their enhancements [7,29,33] have gained tremendous progress over the years, and the gap with Generative Adversarial Nets (GANs) [11] with respect to generative quality has been significantly reduced. The theoretical implication of VAE's success is even far-reaching: high generative quality is achievable without resorting to adversarial training as in GANs. However, VAE has been faced with persistent challenges in practice – given a randomly complex dataset, it is tricky and non-trivial to properly tune the weights between the reconstruction loss, which is responsible for high-quality reconstruction, and the Kullback-Leibler divergence (KLD) loss, which theoretically guarantees a Gaussian and continuous latent space [4]. High-performing generative models shall satisfy both requirements [26]. It's nevertheless popularly believed that enforcing the VAE's Gaussian assumption about the latent space by applying a large weight β on the KLD loss tends to compromise the reconstruction fidelity, leading to a trade-off between the two, as demonstrated in both theory [2,17] and practice [3]. Efforts in solving the problem go primarily in three directions: (a) Increase the complexity of the latent space by using a Gaussian mixture model (GMM) [9,13], or loosen the constraint on the identity covariance matrix [21]. These measures aim to increase the capacity and flexibility of the latent space to allow more complex latent distributions, thus reducing the potential conflicts between the dataset and the prior latent assumption; (b) From an information theory perspective, increase the mutual information between the data and the latent variables explicitly [6,15,27,30,32] or implicitly [8,34]. For example, [8] uses skip connections between the output data space (i.e., the ground truth) and the latent space and proves, both analytically and experimentally, that such skip connections increases the mutual information. These methods are motivated by the observation that the Gaussian assumption about the latent space might prevents the information about the data being efficiently transmitted from the data space to the latent space, and thus the resulting latent variables are not sufficiently informative for a subsequent authentic reconstruction; (c) Most intuitively, tune the weight β of the KLD loss manually (i.e., trial and error) or automatically [3,7,31] during optimization in order to achieve a balance between the reconstruction quality and the latent Gaussian assumption. Specifically, [3,31] applies an increasing weight on the KLD loss during training. A small β at the early stage of training allows the reconstruction loss to prevail, so that the latent variables are informative about the reconstruction. A large β at a later stage attends to the Gaussian assumption. [7] goes a step further and proposes to learn the balancing weight directly. Conceptually, the method presented in our paper is born out of a mixture of (a), (b) and (c), in that our method acknowledges the opposite effects the reconstruction loss and KLD loss may have while training a β-VAE (a, b), and we try to solve the problem by modulating the weight β (c). Among existing methods, it is worth mentioning that the two-stage method proposed in [7] is very similar to our method in form, nevertheless, in essence they differ fundamentally in many aspects[1]: (i) In the first stage, [7] trained a VAE for small reconstruction errors, without requiring the posterior to be close to $\mathcal{N}(\mathbf{0}, I)$, by lowering the dimension of the latent space, whereas we used a large weight β for the KLD loss in this stage to ensure that the posterior maximally approximates $\mathcal{N}(\mathbf{0}, I)$, which nevertheless leads to a large reconstruction error (i.e., low reconstruction fidelity), and the latent space dimension was not accounted for. (ii) In the second stage, [7] trained another VAE using $\mathcal{N}(\mathbf{0}, I)$ as the ground truth latent distribution, and the VAE from both steps are aggregated to achieve a small reconstruction error and a latent distribution close to $\mathcal{N}(\mathbf{0}, I)$ in a unified model. In our method, however, we trained a decoupled decoder with independent parameters using the Gaussian variables from the first stage as input and the data as the ground truth. The decoder is able to converge to a small reconstruction error. [7] and our method are similar in that we try to meet the two criteria of a high-performing generative model i.e., small reconstruction errors and continuous Gaussian latent space $\mathcal{N}(\mathbf{0}, I)$ in two separate stages. However, besides the obvious difference that we realize the two goals in reversed order, the technical and theoretical implications also differ, as will be presented in detail in the following sections.

To put theories into practice, we evaluated the proposed method on a medical dataset – SkullFix [20], which is curated to support researches on 3D human skull reconstruction and completion [22,23,25]. Unlike commonly used VAE benchmarks, such as CIFAR-10, CelebA and MNIST, which are non-medical, relatively lightweight and in 2D, the medical images we used are of high resolution and in 3D. Besides the intended use of VAE for skull reconstruction, the trained VAE is capable of producing a complete skull given as input a defective skull, by slightly modifying the latent variables of the input, similar to a denoising VAE[2] [16]. We can thus establish a connection between conventional AE-based skull shape completion approaches [22–25] and AE-based generative models such as VAE. The contribution and organization of our paper is summarized as follows:

1. We presented a concise review and a careful analysis of the common *Reconstruction-KLD* balance problems in β-VAE, and reformulated the problem in a way such that a solution can be intuitively derived (Sect. 1, 2 and 3).
2. We proposed a simple and intuitive two-stage method to train a β-VAE for maximal generative capability i.e., high-fidelity reconstruction with a continuous and unit Gaussian latent space. The proposed method is free from tuning the hyper-parameter (β) given a specific dataset (Sect. 4).
3. We established a connection between existing AE-based shape completion methods and generative approaches. Results are promising in both quantitative and empirical aspects (Sect. 5).

---

[1] [7] was brought to our attention by a key word search 'two stage vae training', after the completion of our method. An empirical comparison between [7] and our method is provided.

[2] A defective skull can be seen as a complete skull injected with *noise*, i.e., a defect.

4. The proposed method and the results bear empirical implications: an image dataset, even if complex in the image space, can be maximally mapped to a lower dimensional, continuous and unit Gaussian latent space by imposing a large β on the KLD loss. The resulting latent Gaussian variables, even if their distributions are highly overlapped in the latent space, can be mapped to the original image space with high variations and fidelity, by training a decoder decoupled from the KLD loss, i.e., a decoder trained using only the reconstruction loss (Sect. 5 and Sect. 6).

2 β-VAE

In the setting of variational Bayesian inference, the intractable posterior distribution $p(z|x)$ of data x is approximated using a parameterized distribution $q_\theta(z|x)$, by optimizing the Kullback-Leibler divergence (KLD) between the two distributions [19]. Under the setting, $log\,p(x)$ i.e., the log-evidence of the observations x, is lower bounded by a reconstruction term $E_{x \sim q_\theta(z|x)}\,[log\,p_\phi(x|z)]$ and a KLD term $D_{KL}(q_\theta(z|x)||p(z))$:

$$log\,p(x) \geqslant E_{x \sim q_\theta(z|x)}\,[log\,p_\phi(x|z)] - D_{KL}(q_\theta(z|x)||p(z)) \qquad (1)$$

Therefore, the log-evidence $log\,p(x)$ can be maximized by maximizing its lower bound i.e., the right hand side (RHS) of inequality 1, which is commonly known as the evidence lower bound (ELBO). The reconstruction term measures the fidelity of the reconstructed data given latent variables z, and the KLD term regularizes the estimated posterior distribution to be $p(z)$, which is generally assumed to be a standard Gaussian i.e., $z \in \mathcal{N}(0, I)$ in VAE. $q_\theta(z|x)$ and $p_\phi(x|z)$ represent the VAE's encoder and decoder, respectively.

β-VAE [14] imposes a weight β on the KLD term. A large β penalizes the KLD and ensures that the posterior $q_\theta(z|x)$ maximally approximates the prior $p(z) = \mathcal{N}(0, I)$ and has a diagonal covariance matrix. The diagonality of the covariance matrix implies that the dimensions representing the latent features of the input data are uncorrelated, which facilitates deliberate and guided manipulation of the latent variables towards a desired reconstruction.

3   The Antagonistic Mechanism of the Reconstruction Loss and KLD Loss in β-VAE

It is well established, experimentally and potentially theoretically, that β-VAE improves the disentanglement of the latent space desirable for generative tasks by increasing the weight β of the KLD term, which however undermines the reconstructive capability [17]. Here, we interpret the phenomenon by assuming that the reconstruction and KLD term in ELBO are antagonistic and often cannot be jointly optimized for certain hand-curated datasets – the Gaussian assumption about the latent space defies the *inherent* distribution of the dataset, and optimizing KLD exacerbates the reconstruction problem and vice versa.

The problem could be seen more often when it comes to complex and high-dimensional 3D medical images in the medical domain [10]. In this section, we give intuitions of the antagonistic mechanism of the reconstruction and KLD term, from the perspective of information theory and machine learning.

3.1 Information Theory Perspective

The interpretation of VAE's objective (ELBO) can be closely linked with information theory [1,4,5,30]. In [1,4], the authors present intuitions for the connection between β-VAE's objective and the information bottleneck principle [1,5], and consider the posterior distribution $q_\theta(z|x)$ to be a reconstruction bottleneck. Intuitively, since a VAE is trained to reconstruct exactly its input data thanks to the ELBO's reconstruction term, we can think of the unsupervised training as an information transmission process — forcing the posterior $q_\theta(z|x)$ to match a standard Gaussian $\mathcal{N}(\mathbf{0}, I)$ by using a large β causes loss of information about the data in the encoding phase, and as a result, the latent variables z do not carry sufficient information for an authentic reconstruction of the data in the subsequent decoding phase. From an information theory perspective, the KLD between the estimated distribution $q_\theta(z|x)$ and the assumed distribution $p(z)$ can be expressed as the difference between their cross-entropy $H(q_\theta(z|x)||p(z))$ and the entropy of the posterior $H(q_\theta(z|x))$:

$$
\begin{aligned}
D_{KL}(q_\theta(z|x)||p(z)) &= H(q_\theta(z|x), p(z)) - H(q_\theta(z|x)) \\
&= -\int q_\theta(z|x) \log p(z)\, dz - \left(-\int q_\theta(z|x) \log q_\theta(z|x)\, dz\right) \\
&= -\int q_\theta(z|x) \log \frac{p(z)}{q_\theta(z|x)}\, dz
\end{aligned}
\tag{2}
$$

Equation 2 is known as the reverse KLD in VAE optimization. Analogously, the forward KLD is:

$$
\begin{aligned}
D_{KL}(p(z)||q_\theta(z|x)) &= H(p(z), q_\theta(z|x)) - H(p(z)) \\
&= -\int p(z)\log \frac{q_\theta(z|x)}{p(z)}
\end{aligned}
\tag{3}
$$

Note that KLD is not a symmetric measure i.e., $D_{KL}(p(z)||q_\theta(z|x)) \neq D_{KL}(q_\theta(z|x)||p(z))$. Since $p(z) = \mathcal{N}(\mathbf{0}, I)$ is fixed, the forward KLD and cross-entropy are essentially differing only by an additive constant $H(p(z))$. By this, we can connect the optimization of the KLD with the information transmission analogy: the cross-entropy $H(p(z), q_\theta(z|x))$ can be interpreted as the (average) extra amount of information needed to transmit, in order to transmit x from the data space to the latent space z, using the estimated distribution $q_\theta(z|x)$ instead of using $p(z)$. Therefore, optimizing the KLD term minimizes the extra informational efforts, by forcing $q_\theta(z|x) = p(z)$.

Next, we consider the informativeness of the latent variables z towards the input data x, which is modelled by their *mutual information* $\mathcal{I}(x,z)$. Using the reverse KLD in Eq. 2 as an example, the expectation of the KLD term with respect to the data x is given by [17]:

$$
\begin{aligned}
E_{x\sim p(x)}[D_{KL}(q_\theta(z|x)\|p(z))] &= E_{x\sim p(x)}[q_\theta(z|x)\,log\,(\frac{q_\theta(z|x)}{p(z)})] \\
&= E_{x\sim p(x)}E_{\sim q_\theta(z|x)}[log\,\frac{q_\theta(z|x)}{p(z)}] \\
&= E_{x\sim p(x)}E_{\sim q_\theta(z|x)}[log\,\frac{q_\theta(z|x)}{q(z)}+log\,\frac{q(z)}{p(z)}] \quad (4)\\
&= E_{\sim q_\theta(x,z)}[log\,\frac{q_\theta(z|x)}{q(z)}]+E_{\sim q(z)}[log\,\frac{q(z)}{p(z)}] \\
&= I_{\sim q_\theta(z|x)}(x,z)+D_{KL}(q(z)\|p(z))
\end{aligned}
$$

$D_{KL}(q(z)\|p(z)) \geqslant 0$ so that $E_{\sim p(x)}[D_{KL}(q_\theta(z|x)\|p(z))] \geqslant I_{\sim q_\theta(z|x)}(x,z)$. Therefore, the expectation of the KLD term is a upper bound of the mutual information between the data and the latent variables. Consequently, minimizing the KLD also minimizes the mutual information, and hence reduces the informativeness of the latent variables z with respect to the data x. Using a larger β penalizes the KLD and further reduces the mutual information $I(x,z)$ during optimization. In information transmission analogy, a larger β prevents the information being transmitted from the data space to the latent space efficiently.

3.2   Machine Learning Perspective

The antagonistic mechanism can also be interpreted from a machine learning perspective - a large β makes the *latent-to-image* transformation harder to learn. Let the posterior Gaussian distribution be $q_\theta(z|x) = \mathcal{N}(\mu,\Sigma)$. Σ is a diagonal covariance matrix $\Sigma = diag(\sigma_1^2,...,\sigma_d^2)$ and $\mu = (\mu_1,...,\mu_d)$, $z \in R^d$. In the decoding phase of a VAE, a decoder learns to map z sampled from $\mathcal{N}(\mu,\Sigma)^3$ to the image space. An increase in β leads to a larger σ_i, and hence a broader distribution as shown in Fig. 1. When $\{\sigma_i\}_{i=1,2,...,d} \to 0$, the distribution shrinks to a single point, and therefore the decoder essentially is tasked with learning a *one-to-one* mapping as in a conventional autoencoder. When $\{\sigma_i\}_{i=1,2,...,d} \to 1$, the uncertainty of sampling increases as the distribution broadens, and the decoder learns a *many-to-one* mapping i.e., different z sampled from $\mathcal{N}(\mu,\Sigma)$ correspond to the same output, which is significantly harder than learning a *one-to-one* mapping. Learning the *many-to-one* mapping also makes the latent space continuous. Based on the analysis, we present the following observations:

---

[3] Reparameterization: $z \in \mathcal{N}(\mu,\Sigma) => z = \mu + \sigma \odot \varepsilon$, $\varepsilon \in \mathcal{N}(0,I)$.

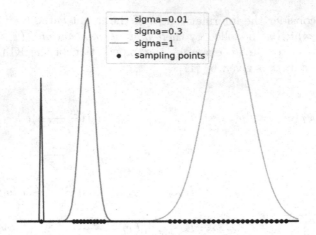

Fig. 1. 1-dimensional Gaussian distributions with different standard deviations *sigma* (σ_i).

Observation 1. *Increasing β in β-VAE increases $\{\sigma_i\}_{i=1,2,...,d}$ and decreases the learnability of the reconstruction problem. Besides, a very high latent dimension d leads to a high sampling uncertainty Ω, which further makes the reconstruction problem harder to learn.*

Explanation: Given $p(z) = \mathcal{N}(\mathbf{0}, I)$, the reverse KLD terms in Eq. 2, which is used in the implementation of β-VAE, can be further decomposed as:

$$
\begin{aligned}
D_{KL}(q_\theta(z|x)||p(z)) &= \frac{1}{2}[log\frac{|I|}{|\Sigma|} - d + tr\{I^{-1}\Sigma\} + (\mathbf{0}-\mu)^T I^{-1}(\mathbf{0}-\mu)] \\
&= \frac{1}{2}[-log|\Sigma| - d + tr\{\Sigma\} + \mu^T\mu] \\
&= -\frac{1}{2}\sum_i^d(1 + log\,\sigma_i^2) + \frac{1}{2}\sum_i^d\sigma_i^2 + \frac{1}{2}\sum_i^d\mu_i^2
\end{aligned}
\tag{5}
$$

In conventional VAE implementations, σ_i and μ_i are connected to the input x via: $(\sigma_1, ..., \sigma_d)^T = \theta_1^T\Phi(x)$ and $\mu^T = \theta_2^T\Phi(x)$. $\Phi(x) \in R^m$ represents the nonlinear feature transform of x, which is realized through several convolutional layers with non-linear activations in VAE's encoder. $\theta_1, \theta_2 \in R^{m \times d}$ represent the weights of two separate linear layers following the convolutional layers. We simplify the explanation by considering that the feature transform Φ is stochastic[4], and hence only the two linear layers i.e., θ_1 and θ_2, need to be optimized.

---

[4] The feature transform learned by the preceding convolutional layers could mostly be replaced by random feature transform [28].

Here, we are only interested in σ_i and θ_1. The gradient of the KLD objective (weighted by β) with respect to θ_1^i, which is the ith column vector of the weight matrix θ_1, is therefore:

$$\nabla \beta D_{KL}(\theta_1^i) = \frac{\partial \beta D_{KL}}{\partial \sigma_i} \frac{\partial \sigma_i}{\partial \theta_1^i} = \beta \frac{\sigma_i^2 - 1}{\sigma_i} \Phi(x) \qquad (6)$$

$\theta_1^i \in R^m$ and $\sigma_i = \Phi(x)\theta_1^i$. The gradient is a vector-valued function i.e., $\nabla \beta D_{KL}(\theta_1^i) : R^m \to R^m$. Obviously, the gradient vector has the same dimension as θ_1^i i.e., $\nabla \beta D_{KL}(\theta_1^i) \in R^m$. We then consider a phase of training when the linear layer's output σ_i is stabilized to range $(0,1)$[5]. To proceed with the explanation, we express the vector notations above using the elements of the vectors, as the following:

$$\theta_1^i = [\theta_1^i(1), \cdots, \theta_1^i(k), \cdots, \theta_1^i(m)] = \{\theta_1^i(k)\}_{k=1,2,\ldots,m}$$

$$\Phi(x) = [\Phi_1(x), \cdots, \Phi_k(x), \cdots, \Phi_m(x)] = \{\Phi_k(x)\}_{k=1,2,\ldots,m}$$

$$\nabla \beta D_{KL}(\theta_1^i) = \begin{bmatrix} \nabla \beta D_{KL}\left(\theta_1^i(1)\right) \\ \cdots \\ \nabla \beta D_{KL}\left(\theta_1^i(k)\right) \\ \cdots \\ \nabla \beta D_{KL}\left(\theta_1^i(m)\right) \end{bmatrix} = \beta \frac{\sigma_i^2 - 1}{\sigma_i} \{\Phi_k(x)\}_{k=1,2,\ldots,m} \qquad (7)$$

$\theta_1^i(k)$ and $\Phi_k(x)$ denote the kth element in θ_1^i and $\Phi(x)$. Therefore, we can express the gradient with respect to a single element of the weight matrix as:

$$\nabla \beta D_{KL}\left(\theta_1^i(k)\right) = \beta \frac{\sigma_i^2 - 1}{\sigma_i} \Phi_k(x) \qquad (8)$$

$\nabla \beta D_{KL}(\theta_1^i(k))$ is a scalar. The summation notation for the vector product $\sigma_i = \Phi(x)\theta_1^i$ is:

$$\sigma_i = \Phi_1(x)\theta_1^i(1) + \cdots + \Phi_k(x)\theta_1^i(k) + \cdots + \Phi_m(x)\theta_1^i(m)$$

$$= \sum_{k=1}^{m} \Phi_k(x)\theta_1^i(k) \in (0,1) \qquad (9)$$

Next, we consider a gradient descent (GD) based optimizer, which updates the elements of the weight matrix according to the following rule:

$$\theta_1^i(k)_{new} = \theta_1^i(k)_{old} - \alpha \nabla \beta D_{KL}\left(\theta_1^i(k)\right) \qquad (10)$$

$\theta_1^i(k)_{new}$ and $\theta_1^i(k)_{old}$ are the new and old values of the weight. $\alpha > 0$ is the learning rate. If $\Phi_k(x) > 0$, then $\nabla \beta D_{KL}\left(\theta_1^i(k)\right) < 0$. According

[5] Due to the *zero-forcing* effect of the reverse KLD (Eq. 2), the estimated posterior distribution $q_\theta(z|x)$ tends to *squeeze* to match $p(z) = \mathcal{N}(\mathbf{0}, I)$. Therefore, it is reasonable to assume that σ_i stays in the range of $(0,1)$ when the optimization process is stabilized. This is a further assumption (simplification) of the explanation.

to the GD optimizer (Eq. 10), the weight increases i.e., $\theta_1^i(k)_{new} > \theta_1^i(k)_{old}$. Therefore, σ_i increases after this update (Eq. 9). Likewise, if $\Phi_k(x) < 0$, then $\nabla \beta D_{KL}\left(\theta_1^i(k)\right) > 0$, and the weight decreases $\theta_1^i(k)_{new} < \theta_1^i(k)_{old}$. In this scenario, σ_i still increases (Eq. 9).

Even though different gradient-based optimizers, such as stochastic gradient descent (SGD), Nesterov's accelerated gradient method, and Adam [18], have different rules for updating the weights, generally the above demonstration still applies (the weights are updated in the direction of negative gradients to minimize a loss function). Equation 6 and Eq. 8 indicate that given $\beta > 1$, the magnitude of the gradient term is larger than when $\beta = 1$. Thus, the increase of σ_i is larger in each iteration during the optimization process compared to using a smaller β. Therefore, larger β in the KLD objective leads to larger σ_i and broader distributions, making the sampling uncertainty of each latent dimension greater. It is also intuitive to understand that the overall uncertainty Ω is positively related to not only the width (σ_i) of the distribution but also to the latent dimension d: $\Omega \propto d, f(\sigma_i)$. $f(\sigma_i) > 1$ is an empirical expression representing the number of points that can be sampled from $\mathcal{N}(\mu_i, \sigma_i)$ during training, and d represents the number of such distributions to sample points from. Hence, the wider the distribution and the larger the latent dimension d, the greater the sampling uncertainty and the lower the learnability of the reconstruction problem. However, in practice, one should be aware of a trade-off between sampling uncertainty and the number of latent dimensions needed to store the necessary amount of information of the data for a reasonable reconstruction, especially when the dimension of the data x is high.

4   Aggregate a Learned Gaussian Posterior with a Decoupled Decoder

One of the important intuitions we derive from the analysis of the antagonistic mechanism in Sect. 3 is that we can enforce a continuous and unit Gaussian latent space by using a large β. Conversely, we can maximally release the reconstructive capability of a VAE by lifting the Gaussian constraint on the latent space (i.e., by setting $\beta = 0$). These intuitions naturally lead to a two-stage training method, which meets the two requirements in two separate steps. A model satisfying both criteria can be aggregated using the separate results:

$$z \sim q_\theta(z|x), x \sim p_\phi(x|z) \tag{11}$$

Unlike in VAE where the encoder $q_\theta(z|x)$ and decoder $p_\phi(x|z)$ is optimized jointly, we first learn a posterior distribution $q_\theta(z|x)$ that maximally approximates $\mathcal{N}(0, I)$, and then we sample the approximate Gaussian variables from the learned distributions $z \sim q_\theta(z|x)$, and finally we use a decoder decoupled from the VAE framework (and hence the KLD constraint) to learn a distribution of the data conditioned on the sampled Gaussian variables. The reconstruction can thus be $x \sim p_\phi(x|z)$.

Using a VAE to Learn $q_\theta(z|x)$

A posterior $q_\theta(z|x)$ that satisfies the Gaussian assumption is easily learned by imposing a large β on the KLD loss. Aside from this, it is safe to assume that since the KLD term is optimized simultaneously with a reconstruction term under a VAE framework, the reconstruction term is likely to have an influence on the latent space/variables as well. In other words, latent variables z sampled from $q_\theta(z|x)$ likely carry some information about the image space[6].

Using a Decoder to Learn $p_\phi(x|z)$

Empirically, we can provide a convergence guarantee for the decoder by revisiting the fundamental implications of GANs: a vanilla decoder (i.e., the GANs' generator) is capable of learning a transformation between *completely random Gaussian variables* and authentic (natural) images when combined with a discriminator via adversarial training [11]. We leverage this insight and present the following empirical conjecture:

Conjecture 1. A vanilla decoder can learn such *Gaussian-to-image* transformation through conventional natural training, if the Gaussian variables already carry some information about the images, i.e., the Gaussian variables are not complete random with respect to the image space.

This conjecture can be understood empirically. We require that the input Gaussian variables of a generative model are *aware* of the image space instead of being complete random as in GANs, and expect that such variables can be mapped to the image space with adequate quality using only natural training, without resorting to GANs' adversarial training.

We already showed previously that the latent variables $z \sim q_\theta(z|x)$ satisfy the Gaussian assumption and are *aware* of the image space, so that we can apply Conjecture 1 in our method. A decoder decoupled from the VAE framework can be used to learn $p_\phi(x|z)$, by optimizing only the reconstruction term. To sum up, the first stage of training aims for a continuous and Gaussian latent space, and the second stage aims for an optimal reconstruction.

5 Application to Skull Reconstruction and Shape Completion

In this section, we evaluate the proposed two-stage VAE training method on the SkullFix dataset [20]. The dataset originally contains 100 complete skulls and their corresponding cranially defective skulls for training. For our VAE experiments, we additionally created 100 skulls with facial defects out of the complete

---

[6] Here, *"carry some information about the image space"* is only an empirical statement, and is used to contrast against *completely random Gaussian variables* in GANs.

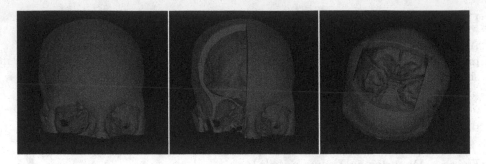

Fig. 2. Illustration of a complete skull (left) and skulls with facial (middle) and cranial (right) defects.

skulls, amounting to 300 training samples, and downsampled the images from the original $512 \times 512 \times Z$ (Z is the axial dimension of the skull images) to $256 \times 256 \times 128$. Figure 2 shows a complete skull and its two corresponding defective skulls. We train a VAE on the 300 training samples[7], following the two-stage protocol:

1. The VAE is trained for 200 epochs with $\beta = 100$.
2. We fix the encoding and sampling part of the trained VAE from the previous step and train a separate decoupled decoder for *latent-to-image* transformation, for 1200 epochs.

The VAE's encoder and decoder in Step 1 are composed of six convolutional and deconvolutional layers, respectively. The latent dimension d is set to 32. The latent vectors $\mu \in R^{32}$ and $(\sigma_1^2, ..., \sigma_{32}^2)$ come from two linear layers connecting the encoder's output. The decoder in Step 2 is a conventional 6-layer deconvolutional network that upsamples the 32-dimensional latent variables from Step 1 to the image space ($R^{32} \rightarrow R^{256 \times 256 \times 128}$). For comparison, we also train the VAE in Step 1 with $\beta = 0.0001$ for 200 epochs. In all experiments, Dice loss [22] is chosen for the ELBO's reconstruction term. The VAE and related methods are implemented using the MONAI (Medical Open Network for Artificial Intelligence) framework (https://monai.io/).

5.1 Training Curves

Figure 3 shows the training curves of the Dice and KLD loss of the regular VAE and decoupled decoder. The curves conform to our analysis and intuitions:

1. With $\beta = 0.0001$, the reconstruction loss prevails and can decrease to a desired small value, while the KLD loss increases (i.e., antagonistic), which guarantees a high reconstruction fidelity by largely *ignoring* the latent Gaussian assumption.

---

[7] Each sample is used both as input and ground truth as in an autoencoder.

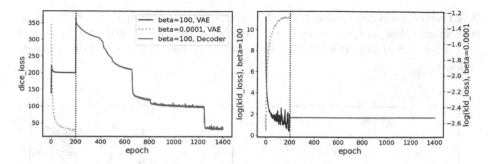

Fig. 3. Training curves of the VAE and the decoupled decoder regarding Dice (left) and KLD (right) loss. For the KLD loss curve, two y-axis with different y-limits are used for $\beta = 100$ and $\beta = 0.0001$.

2. With $\beta = 100$, the KLD loss decreases while the reconstruction loss increases. The VAE guarantees a continuous Gaussian latent space while failing in authentic reconstruction[8]. Besides, using $\beta = 100$ keeps the reconstruction loss from further decreasing (i.e., antagonistic. See Fig. 9 in Appendix A).
3. The latent Gaussian variables generated with $\beta = 100$ can be mapped to the original image space at similar reconstruction loss as with $\beta = 0.0001$, by using an independently trained decoder, implying that even if the distribution of these Gaussian variables might be heavily overlapping in the latent space, the decoder is still able to produce varied reconstructions if properly/ sufficiently trained (e.g., train for 1200 epochs). The results conform to our Conjecture 1.
4. We can obtain a generative model that maximally satisfies the VAE's Gaussian assumption about the latent space while still preserving decent reconstruction fidelity by aggregating the encoder of the VAE trained with $\beta = 100$ and an independent decoder trained for *latent-to-image* transformation.

It is important to note that, for different training epochs in Step 2, the input of the decoder corresponding to a skull sample can vary due to stochastic sampling $z \in \mathcal{N}(\mu, \Sigma)$, just like in a complete VAE, to ensure that every variable from the continuous latent space can be mapped to a reasonable reconstruction (i.e., *many-to-one* mapping). One can see that the two-stage VAE training method does not involve tuning the hyper-parameter β, except that we need to empirically choose a large value e.g., $\beta = 100$ in our experiments, for Step 1, and is applicable to other datasets out of the box. Besides, the decoder in Step

---

[8] We observe that the VAE always gives unvaried output under $\beta = 100$, and the output preserves the general skull shape but lacks anatomical (e.g., facial) details. See Fig. 10 (B) in Appendix A for a reconstruction result under $\beta = 100$. This is due to the fact that large β broadens the distributions of the latent variables, making different distributions maximally overlap. This tricks the decoder to believe that all latent variables originate from the same distribution, hence giving unvaried reconstruction [4].

2 is trained for 1200 epochs until the reconstruction (Dice) loss can converge to a small value comparable to a regular VAE under $\beta = 0.0001$, indicating, as discussed in Sect. 3.2, that the *latent-to-image* transformation is more difficult to learn.

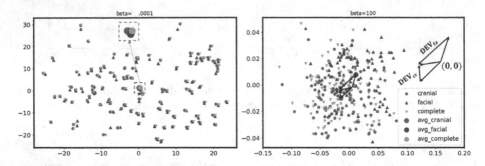

Fig. 4. The distribution of the latent variables given $\beta = 0.0001$ (regular VAE, left) and $\beta = 100$ (regular VAE, right). The large filled circles represent the centroids of the respective skull classes. The black arrows on the RHS of the plot point from the origin $(0,0)$ to the centroids, and from the two defective centroids (red and blue) to the complete center (green). (Color figure online)

5.2   Skull Reconstruction and Skull Shape Completion

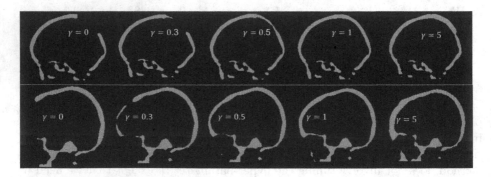

Fig. 5. Skull shape completion given $\beta = 0.0001$ (regular VAE) and different γ (see Eq. 13). The first and second row shows the shape completion results given a cranial and facial defect, respectively.

In this section, we use the trained regular VAE (under $\beta = 0.0001$) and the aggregated VAE (regular VAE under $\beta = 100$ aggregated with the trained decoupled decoder) for skull reconstruction and skull shape completion. By skull reconstruction, we evaluate how well the VAE reproduces its input, and by skull shape completion, we use the VAE to generate complete skulls from defective inputs as in [25], even if it is not explicitly trained for this purpose. Figure 4 shows the distribution of the latent variables z of the three skull classes given $\beta = 0.0001$ (regular VAE) and $\beta = 100$ (regular VAE). For illustration purposes, the dimension of the latent variables is reduced from 32 to 2 using principal component analysis (PCA). We can see that for $\beta = 0.0001$, a complete skull and its corresponding two defective skulls are closer to each other than to other skull samples in the latent space, and these variables as a whole are not clustered based on skull classes. For $\beta = 100$, we can see that the variables as a whole are packed around the origin $(0,0)$ of the latent space, and are clustered based on different skull classes – complete skulls, skulls with cranial and facial defects. The *cluster-forming* phenomenon indicates that the ELBO's reconstruction term enforces some information related to the image space on the latent variables (Conjecture 1). The results also generally conform to the VAE's Gaussian assumption $z \in \mathcal{N}(\mathbf{0}, I)$, and sampling randomly from the continuous latent space has a higher probability for a reasonable reconstruction than from a nearly discrete latent space ($\beta = 0.0001$). However, unlike the MNIST dataset commonly used in VAE-related researches, the skull clusters are heavily overlapping, with the cluster of the facial defects moderately deviating from the other two. This is also understandable, since we cannot guarantee that the skulls are differently distributed in a latent space while handcrafting the defects from the complete skulls in the image space.

Table 1. Quantitative evaluation results (Dice similarity coefficient - DSC) of skull reconstruction (REC) and skull shape completion (CMP) given $\beta = 0.0001$ (regular VAE) and $\beta = 100$ (aggregated VAE).

β	Reconstruction (REC)			Completion (CMP)	
	Cranial	Facial	Complete	Cranial	Facial
$\beta = 0.0001$ (regular VAE)	0.9153	0.9215	0.9199	0.9189	0.9072
$\beta = 100$ (aggregated VAE)	0.9076	0.9094	0.9127	0.8978	0.7934

For skull reconstruction, these latent variables are mapped to the image space using the respective decoders. For skull shape completion, we define the following: let the latent variables of the complete skulls, facially and cranially defective skulls from the training samples be $\mathbf{z}^{co}$, $\mathbf{z}^{fa}$ and $\mathbf{z}^{cr}$. We therefore compute the average deviation of the defective skulls (facial: DEV_{fa}; cranial:

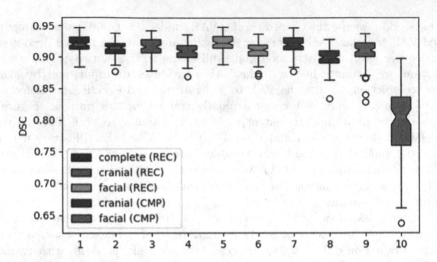

Fig. 6. DSC boxplots for skull reconstruction (REC) and skull shape completion (CMP) given $\beta = 0.0001$ (regular VAE, left) and $\beta = 100$ (aggregated VAE, right).

DEV_{cr}) from their corresponding complete skulls as:

$$DEV_{cr} = \frac{1}{N} \sum_i^N (\mathbf{z}_i^{co} - \mathbf{z}_i^{cr}) = \frac{1}{N} \sum_i^N \mathbf{z}_i^{co} - \frac{1}{N} \sum_i^N \mathbf{z}_i^{cr}$$

$$DEV_{fa} = \frac{1}{N} \sum_i^N (\mathbf{z}_i^{co} - \mathbf{z}_i^{fa}) = \frac{1}{N} \sum_i^N \mathbf{z}_i^{co} - \frac{1}{N} \sum_i^N \mathbf{z}_i^{fa} \tag{12}$$

$N = 100$ is the number of samples of a skull class. Since $\frac{1}{N} \sum_i^N \mathbf{z}_i^{co}$, $\frac{1}{N} \sum_i^N \mathbf{z}_i^{cr}$ and $\frac{1}{N} \sum_i^N \mathbf{z}_i^{fa}$ essentially compute the centroids of the respective skull clusters, DEV_{fa} and DEV_{cr} in Eq. 12 can be interpreted intuitively as the two deviation vectors shown in Fig. 4 or the *implant*. In this sense, skull shape completion means interpolating between the defective and complete skull classes. Given a defective skull whose latent variable is $\mathbf{z}_{ts}$ as a test sample, the latent variable that decodes to a complete skull corresponding to the defective test sample can be computed as (vector arithmetic):

$$z^{cr \to co} = \mathbf{z}_{ts} + \gamma DEV_{cr}$$

$$z^{fa \to co} = \mathbf{z}_{ts} + \gamma DEV_{fa} \tag{13}$$

$\gamma \in \mathcal{R}$ controls the extent of completion. With $\gamma = 0$, we expect that the resulting latent variable would be decoded to the original defective sample (i.e., skull reconstruction). With $\gamma = 1$, we expect that decoding the latent variable

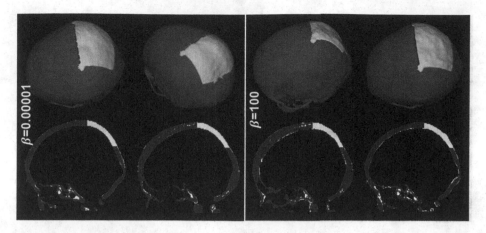

Fig. 7. Cranial shape completion results given $\beta = 0.0001$ (regular VAE) and $\beta = 100$ (aggregated VAE). The *implants* shown in yellow correspond to the deviation vectors DEV_{cr} in Eq. 12. (Color figure online)

yields a complete skull (i.e., skull shape completion). Figure 5 shows the decoding results given different γ and $\beta = 0.0001$. Given $0 < \gamma < 1$, we can see the gradual evolution of the output (from defective to complete). Similar results are observed for $\beta = 100$ (aggregated VAE). Besides, the VAE can extrapolate the output by *thickening* the *implant* given $\gamma > 1$, as can be seen in Fig. 5. Table 1 and Fig. 6 show the quantitative evaluation results for skull reconstruction and skull shape completion. We measure the agreement between the input and the reconstruction using Dice similarity coefficient (DSC). We can see that the reconstruction accuracy obtained under a heavy regularization of the latent space (i.e., $\beta = 100$, aggregated VAE) is comparable to that under a weak regularizer (i.e., $\beta = 0.0001$, regular VAE), indicating that the Gaussian variables can be used for decent skull reconstruction using the decoupled decoder, without resorting to adversarial training as in GANs (Conjecture 1). However, for $\beta = 100$, we see a noticeable performance drop in the shape completion task on facial defects. An educated guess of the cause, based on known results reported in Table 1 and Fig. 6, is that in the latent space created by using $\beta = 100$, the variables from the complete and cranially defective skulls are heavily overlapped, while the latent variables of the facially defective skulls are obviously deviating (Fig. 4). As a result, the magnitude of the deviation vector representing the facial *implant* (Eq. 12) is much higher compared to that of the cranial deviation vector. Figure 7 and Fig. 8 show examples of skull shape completion results in 2D and 3D under $\beta = 0.0001$ (regular VAE) and $\beta = 100$ (aggregated VAE), for the cranial and facial defects. The results are obtained based on Eq. 13 given $\gamma = 1$. We further obtain the *implant* by taking the *difference* between the decoding results i.e., completed skulls and the defective input in the image space. For conventional AE-based skull shape completion results, we refer the readers to Fig. 11 in Appendix B.

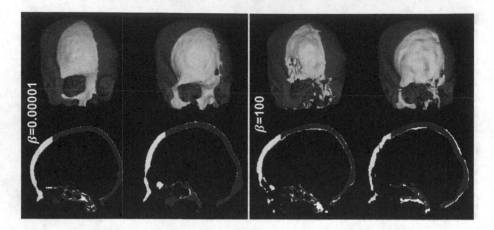

Fig. 8. Facial shape completion results given $\beta = 0.0001$ (regular VAE) and $\beta = 100$ (aggregated VAE). The *implants* shown in yellow correspond to the deviation vectors DEV_{fa} in Eq. 12. (Color figure online)

6   Discussion and Conclusion

An explicit separation of the prediction accuracy and network complexity in the loss function of variational inference allows one to manipulate the optimization process by adjusting the weights of the two loss terms [12]. In VAE, the reconstruction term and the KLD term corresponds to the *accuracy* and *complexity*, respectively. In this paper, we evaluated the influence of the KLD weight β on the reconstructive and generative capability of β-VAE, using a skull dataset. We considered three scenarios: $\beta = 0.0001$ (low network complexity), $\beta = 100$ (high network complexity), and an aggregate of the posterior distribution from $\beta = 100$ and a decoupled decoder independently trained for skull reconstruction. Experiments reveal that even if the KLD loss increases during training under $\beta = 0.0001$, it is able to stabilize at some point (Fig. 3). As expected, the resulting latent space is non-continuous (Fig. 4). However, the tendency of the latent variables assembling around the origin $(0,0)$ is noticeable, which shows the (weak) influence of the KLD loss. This could explain the reason why we can still interpolate smoothly among skull classes on a local scale given $\beta = 0.0001$, and perform skull shape completion by manipulating the latent variables (Fig. 5, Eq. 12, Eq. 13). The reconstructive capability of the network can also be fully exploited by using the small β − an advantage (i.e., small reconstruction error) which appears to outweigh the disadvantages (i.e., non-continuous latent space) on this particular dataset and task. In comparison, we realize a globally continuous, maximally unit Gaussian latent space by using $\beta = 100$ (Fig. 4), and a small reconstruction loss by training a separate decoder decoupled from the KLD loss (Fig. 3). However, the shape completion performance on facial defects is suboptimal compared to that on cranial defects and skull reconstruction (Table 1 and Fig. 6). Empirically, the results could be improved by reformulating the definition of the cluster centroids in Eq. 12, so that the centroids of different skull clusters are closer. The problem is not unexpectable, since exploiting the disentanglement features of the latent space is often a delicate issue [10]. Last but not least, we would like to point out one of the major limitations of our current work: the proposed two-stage method in Sect. 4 is largely suggested by empirical analysis. Rigorous theoretical guarantee has yet been provided in its current form. Future work demonstrating or refuting the universal applicability and theoretical guarantee of the method is to be conducted. Besides, Observation 1 and Conjecture 1 as well as their explanation presented in this paper are also empirical. A formal expression of the Rademacher complexity involving the latent dimension d, the weight β and the variance σ_i for the learnability of the reconstruction problem (Observation 1), as well as a theoretical proof of the convergence guarantee for the decoupled decoder (Conjecture 1) is also desired in future work.

Appendix A   VAE Training Curve (1200 Epochs) under $\beta = 100$

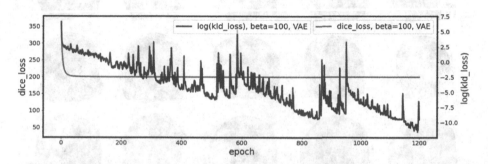

Fig. 9. Training a regular VAE (the same VAE used in Sect. 5) for 1200 epochs under $\beta = 100$. The curve shows the Dice and KLD loss for the entire training process.

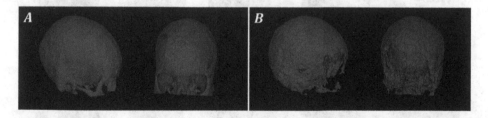

Fig. 10. Reconstruction results from (A) the aggregated VAE, and (B) a regular VAE trained for 1200 epochs under $\beta = 100$.

Figure 9 shows the training curve of the Dice and KLD loss under $\beta = 100$. We can see that after 1200 epochs (training took approximately 120 h on a desktop

PC with a 24 GB NVIDIA GeForce RTX 3090 GPU and an AMD Ryzen 9, 5900X 12-Core CPU), the reconstruction (Dice) loss is still not able to decrease to a desirable small value. As a result, the VAE gives poor reconstruction (Fig. 10 (B)), and the output is unvaried given different input skulls. In contrast, the reconstruction loss of the decoupled decoder can converge to around 30 after 1200 epochs (Fig. 3), and thus the aggregated VAE can produce desirable and varied reconstructions, as can be seen from Fig. 10 (A).

Appendix B   AE-Based Skull Shape Completion

In this appendix, we show results of an AE-based shape completion method for facial defects. The AE used here is the same as N_1 in [24], and is implemented in

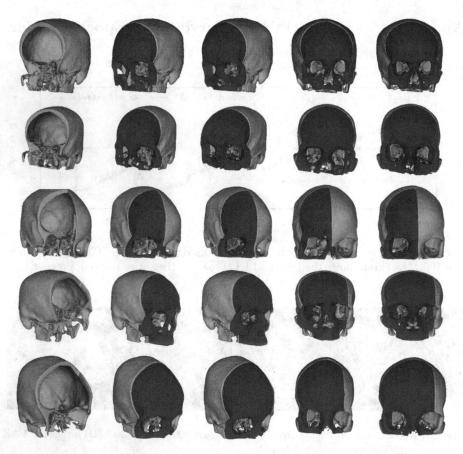

Fig. 11. Skull shape completion results for facial defects, obtained using a conventional autoencoder from [24]. The first column shows the input. The second and fourth column show the predictions from two different views. The third and last column show the corresponding ground truth.

tensorflow (https://www.tensorflow.org/). Unlike VAE, the AE is trained explicitly for skull shape completion, with the input being a facially defective skull and the output being the corresponding complete skull. Qualitative results are shown in Fig. 11. It is obvious and expected that the completion results are much better than those of VAE, since the AE is explicitly trained for the completion task. Furthermore, bear in mind that skull completion (especially for facial defects) is an ill-posed problem, and the network is trained to produce a complete skull that is anatomically plausible but not necessarily resembling the ground truth.

Appendix C   Matrix Notation for $\triangledown \beta D_{KL}(\theta_1)$

The partial derivative of the KLD loss with respect to a single element of the weight matrix θ_1 (i.e., Eq. 8 in the main manuscript) can be more compactly derived and expressed using matrix calculus. To this end, we define:

$$\theta_1 = \begin{bmatrix} \theta_1^{11} & \theta_1^{21} & \theta_1^{31} & \cdots & \theta_1^{m1} \\ \theta_1^{12} & \theta_1^{22} & \theta_1^{32} & \cdots & \theta_1^{m2} \\ \vdots & \vdots & \vdots & \ddots & \vdots \\ \theta_1^{1d} & \theta_1^{2d} & \theta_1^{3d} & \cdots & \theta_1^{md} \end{bmatrix}^T \in R^{m \times d} \tag{C.1}$$

$$\begin{aligned} \sigma = \theta_1^T \cdot \Phi(x) &= \begin{bmatrix} \theta_1^{11} & \theta_1^{21} & \theta_1^{31} & \cdots & \theta_1^{m1} \\ \theta_1^{12} & \theta_1^{22} & \theta_1^{32} & \cdots & \theta_1^{m2} \\ \vdots & \vdots & \vdots & \ddots & \vdots \\ \theta_1^{1d} & \theta_1^{2d} & \theta_1^{3d} & \cdots & \theta_1^{md} \end{bmatrix} \cdot \begin{bmatrix} \Phi_1(x) \\ \Phi_2(x) \\ \vdots \\ \Phi_m(x) \end{bmatrix} \\ &= \begin{bmatrix} \sum_{k=1}^{m} \theta_1^{k1} \Phi_k(x) \\ \sum_{k=1}^{m} \theta_1^{k2} \Phi_k(x) \\ \vdots \\ \sum_{k=1}^{m} \theta_1^{kd} \Phi_k(x) \end{bmatrix} = \begin{bmatrix} \sigma_1 \\ \sigma_2 \\ \vdots \\ \sigma_d \end{bmatrix} \end{aligned} \tag{C.2}$$

Based on Eq. 5 in the main manuscript and the above matrix notations, we can calculate the derivative of the KLD loss with respect to θ_1 directly:

$$
\nabla \beta D_{KL}(\theta_1) = \beta
\begin{bmatrix}
\frac{\partial D_{KL}}{\partial \theta_1^{11}} & \frac{\partial D_{KL}}{\partial \theta_1^{21}} & \frac{\partial D_{KL}}{\partial \theta_1^{31}} & \cdots & \frac{\partial D_{KL}}{\partial \theta_1^{m1}} \\
\frac{\partial D_{KL}}{\partial \theta_1^{12}} & \frac{\partial D_{KL}}{\partial \theta_1^{22}} & \frac{\partial D_{KL}}{\partial \theta_1^{32}} & \cdots & \frac{\partial D_{KL}}{\partial \theta_1^{m2}} \\
\vdots & \vdots & \vdots & \ddots & \vdots \\
\frac{\partial D_{KL}}{\partial \theta_1^{1d}} & \frac{\partial D_{KL}}{\partial \theta_1^{2d}} & \frac{\partial D_{KL}}{\partial \theta_1^{3d}} & \cdots & \frac{\partial D_{KL}}{\partial \theta_1^{md}}
\end{bmatrix}^T
$$

$$
= \beta
\begin{bmatrix}
\frac{\partial D_{KL}}{\partial \sigma_1}\frac{\sigma_1}{\partial \theta_1^{11}} & \frac{\partial D_{KL}}{\partial \sigma_1}\frac{\sigma_1}{\partial \theta_1^{21}} & \frac{\partial D_{KL}}{\partial \sigma_1}\frac{\sigma_1}{\partial \theta_1^{31}} & \cdots & \frac{\partial D_{KL}}{\partial \sigma_1}\frac{\sigma_1}{\partial \theta_1^{m1}} \\
\frac{\partial D_{KL}}{\partial \sigma_2}\frac{\sigma_2}{\partial \theta_1^{12}} & \frac{\partial D_{KL}}{\partial \sigma_2}\frac{\sigma_2}{\partial \theta_1^{22}} & \frac{\partial D_{KL}}{\partial \sigma_2}\frac{\sigma_2}{\partial \theta_1^{32}} & \cdots & \frac{\partial D_{KL}}{\partial \sigma_2}\frac{\sigma_2}{\partial \theta_1^{m2}} \\
\vdots & \vdots & \vdots & \ddots & \vdots \\
\frac{\partial D_{KL}}{\partial \sigma_d}\frac{\sigma_d}{\partial \theta_1^{1d}} & \frac{\partial D_{KL}}{\partial \sigma_d}\frac{\sigma_d}{\partial \theta_1^{2d}} & \frac{\partial D_{KL}}{\partial \sigma_d}\frac{\sigma_d}{\partial \theta_1^{3d}} & \cdots & \frac{\partial D_{KL}}{\partial \sigma_d}\frac{\sigma_d}{\partial \theta_1^{md}}
\end{bmatrix}^T
$$

$$
= \beta
\begin{bmatrix}
\frac{\sigma_1^2-1}{\sigma_1}\Phi_1(x) & \frac{\sigma_1^2-1}{\sigma_1}\Phi_2(x) & \frac{\sigma_1^2-1}{\sigma_1}\Phi_3(x) & \cdots & \frac{\sigma_1^2-1}{\sigma_1}\Phi_m(x) \\
\frac{\sigma_2^2-1}{\sigma_2}\Phi_1(x) & \frac{\sigma_2^2-1}{\sigma_2}\Phi_2(x) & \frac{\sigma_2^2-1}{\sigma_2}\Phi_3(x) & \cdots & \frac{\sigma_2^2-1}{\sigma_2}\Phi_m(x) \\
\vdots & \vdots & \vdots & \ddots & \vdots \\
\frac{\sigma_d^2-1}{\sigma_d}\Phi_1(x) & \frac{\sigma_d^2-1}{\sigma_d}\Phi_2(x) & \frac{\sigma_d^2-1}{\sigma_d}\Phi_3(x) & \cdots & \frac{\sigma_d^2-1}{\sigma_d}\Phi_m(x)
\end{bmatrix}^T \in R^{m \times d}
$$

$$(C.3)$$

We define θ_1^{ki} as the weight at the kth row and i^{th} column in the weight matrix θ_1. Then, the partial derivative of the KLD loss with respect to θ_1^{ki} is simply $\frac{\partial D_{KL}}{\partial \theta_1^{ki}} = \beta \frac{\sigma_i^2-1}{\sigma_i}\Phi_k(x)$, which is the same as Eq. 8 in the main manuscript.

References

1. Alemi, A.A., Fischer, I., Dillon, J.V., Murphy, K.: Deep variational information bottleneck. arXiv preprint arXiv:1612.00410 (2016)
2. Asperti, A., Trentin, M.: Balancing reconstruction error and kullback-leibler divergence in variational autoencoders. IEEE Access **8**, 199440–199448 (2020)
3. Bowman, S.R., Vilnis, L., Vinyals, O., Dai, A.M., Jozefowicz, R., Bengio, S.: Generating sentences from a continuous space. arXiv preprint arXiv:1511.06349 (2015)
4. Burgess, C.P., et al.: Understanding disentangling in $\beta - vae$. arXiv preprint arXiv:1804.03599 (2018)
5. Chechik, G., Globerson, A., Tishby, N., Weiss, Y.: Information bottleneck for gaussian variables. In: Advances in Neural Information Processing Systems, vol. 16 (2003)
6. Chen, X., Duan, Y., Houthooft, R., Schulman, J., Sutskever, I., Abbeel, P.: InfoGAN: interpretable representation learning by information maximizing generative adversarial nets. In: Advances in Neural Information Processing Systems, vol. 29 (2016)
7. Dai, B., Wipf, D.: Diagnosing and enhancing vae models. arXiv preprint arXiv:1903.05789 (2019)
8. Dieng, A.B., Kim, Y., Rush, A.M., Blei, D.M.: Avoiding latent variable collapse with generative skip models. In: The 22nd International Conference on Artificial Intelligence and Statistics, pp. 2397–2405. PMLR (2019)

9. Dilokthanakul, N., et al.: Deep unsupervised clustering with gaussian mixture variational autoencoders. arXiv preprint arXiv:1611.02648 (2016)
10. Fragemann, J., Ardizzone, L., Egger, J., Kleesiek, J.: Review of disentanglement approaches for medical applications-towards solving the gordian knot of generative models in healthcare. arXiv preprint arXiv:2203.11132 (2022)
11. Goodfellow, I., et al.: Generative adversarial nets. In: Advances in Neural Information Processing Systems, vol. 27 (2014)
12. Graves, A.: Practical variational inference for neural networks. In: Advances in Neural Information Processing Systems, vol. 24 (2011)
13. Guo, C., Zhou, J., Chen, H., Ying, N., Zhang, J., Zhou, D.: Variational autoencoder with optimizing gaussian mixture model priors. IEEE Access **8**, 43992–44005 (2020)
14. Higgins, I., et al.: β-VAE: learning basic visual concepts with a constrained variational framework (2016)
15. Hoffman, M.D., Johnson, M.J.: ELBO surgery: yet another way to carve up the variational evidence lower bound. In: Workshop in Advances in Approximate Bayesian Inference, NIPS, vol. 1 (2016)
16. Im Im, D., Ahn, S., Memisevic, R., Bengio, Y.: Denoising criterion for variational auto-encoding framework. In: Proceedings of the AAAI Conference on Artificial Intelligence, vol. 31 (2017)
17. Kim, H., Mnih, A.: Disentangling by factorising. In: International Conference on Machine Learning, pp. 2649–2658. PMLR (2018)
18. Kingma, D.P., Ba, J.: Adam: a method for stochastic optimization. arXiv preprint arXiv:1412.6980 (2014)
19. Kingma, D.P., Welling, M.: Auto-encoding variational bayes. arXiv preprint arXiv:1312.6114 (2013)
20. Kodym, O., et al.: Skullbreak/skullfix-dataset for automatic cranial implant design and a benchmark for volumetric shape learning tasks. Data Brief **35**, 106902 (2021)
21. Langley, J., Monteiro, M., Jones, C., Pawlowski, N., Glocker, B.: Structured uncertainty in the observation space of variational autoencoders. arXiv preprint arXiv:2205.12533 (2022)
22. Li, J., et al.: Automatic skull defect restoration and cranial implant generation for cranioplasty. Med. Image Anal. 102171 (2021)
23. Li, J., Gsaxner, C., Pepe, A., Schmalstieg, D., Kleesiek, J., Egger, J.: Sparse Convolutional Neural Networks for Medical Image Analysis (2022). https://doi.org/10.36227/techrxiv.19137518.v2
24. Li, J., Pepe, A., Gsaxner, C., Campe, G., Egger, J.: A baseline approach for AutoImplant: the MICCAI 2020 cranial implant design challenge. In: Syeda-Mahmood, T., et al. (eds.) CLIP/ML-CDS -2020. LNCS, vol. 12445, pp. 75–84. Springer, Cham (2020). https://doi.org/10.1007/978-3-030-60946-7_8
25. Li, J., et al.: Autoimplant 2020-first MICCAI challenge on automatic cranial implant design. IEEE Trans. Med. Imaging **40**(9), 2329–2342 (2021)
26. Makhzani, A., Shlens, J., Jaitly, N., Goodfellow, I., Frey, B.: Adversarial autoencoders. arXiv preprint arXiv:1511.05644 (2015)
27. Qian, D., Cheung, W.K.: Enhancing variational autoencoders with mutual information neural estimation for text generation. In: Proceedings of the 2019 Conference on Empirical Methods in Natural Language Processing and the 9th International Joint Conference on Natural Language Processing (EMNLP-IJCNLP), pp. 4047–4057 (2019)
28. Rahimi, A., Recht, B.: Random features for large-scale kernel machines. In: Advances in Neural Information Processing Systems, vol. 20 (2007)

29. Razavi, A., Van den Oord, A., Vinyals, O.: Generating diverse high-fidelity images with VQ-VAE-2. In: Advances in Neural Information Processing Systems, vol. 32 (2019)
30. Rezaabad, A.L., Vishwanath, S.: Learning representations by maximizing mutual information in variational autoencoders. In: 2020 IEEE International Symposium on Information Theory (ISIT), pp. 2729–2734. IEEE (2020)
31. Sandfort, V., Yan, K., Graffy, P.M., Pickhardt, P.J., Summers, R.M.: Use of variational autoencoders with unsupervised learning to detect incorrect organ segmentations at CT. Radiol. Artif. Intell. 3(4) (2021)
32. Serdega, A., Kim, D.S.: VMI-VAE: variational mutual information maximization framework for VAE with discrete and continuous priors. arXiv preprint arXiv:2005.13953 (2020)
33. Van Den Oord, A., Vinyals, O., et al.: Neural discrete representation learning. In: Advances in Neural Information Processing Systems, vol. 30 (2017)
34. Zhao, S., Song, J., Ermon, S.: InfoVAE: balancing learning and inference in variational autoencoders. In: Proceedings of the AAAI Conference on Artificial Intelligence, vol. 33, pp. 5885–5892 (2019)

Normalizing-Flow-Based Approaches

Disentangling Factors of Morphological Variation in an Invertible Brain Aging Model

Matthias Wilms[1,2,3](✉), Pauline Mouches[1,2,3], Jordan J. Bannister[1,2,3], Sönke Langner[4], and Nils D. Forkert[1,2,3]

[1] Department of Radiology, University of Calgary, Calgary, Canada
matthias.wilms@ucalgary.ca
[2] Hotchkiss Brain Institute, University of Calgary, Calgary, Canada
[3] Alberta Children's Hospital Research Institute, University of Calgary, Calgary, Canada
[4] Institute for Diagnostic and Interventional Radiology, Pediatric and Neuroradiology, University Medical Center Rostock, Rostock, Germany

Abstract. Neuroimaging-based machine learning models are widely employed to analyze healthy brain aging and its pathological deviations. This includes regression models that estimate a brain's biological age using structural MR images, generative models that capture the conditional distribution of aging-related brain morphology changes, and hybrid generative-inferential models that handle both tasks. Generative models are useful when systematically analyzing the influence that different semantic factors have on brain morphology. Within this context, this paper builds upon a recently proposed normalizing flow-based, generative-inferential brain aging model (iBAM) that uses supervision to disentangle age and age-unrelated identity information of a subject's brain morphology in its structured latent space. We analyze the effects adding sex as an additional supervised factor to iBAM has on the latent space when using real data. Moreover, we propose to learn an identity part that is ordered with respect to the amount of morphological variability covered. Our results on T1 images from more than 5000 healthy subjects show that iBAM is able to successfully disentangle age and sex from the identity information using supervision. Furthermore, the identity part is ordered, which aids efficient exploration and summarization of inter-subject variations.

Keywords: Brain aging · Normalizing flows · Disentanglement

1 Introduction

Over the years, many neuroimaging-based machine learning models for analyzing the process of healthy brain aging and its potentially pathological deviations have been proposed. This includes a multitude of CNN-based regression models that estimate a brain's biological age using (structural) MRI data (e.g.,

J. Fragemann et al. (Eds.): MAD 2022, LNCS 13823, pp. 95–107, 2023.
https://doi.org/10.1007/978-3-031-25046-0_8

[8,19,22,24]). A positive difference between a patient's biological and known chronological brain age is often assumed to be an indicator for neurodegenerative disorders such as Alzheimer's disease [9]. A considerable amount of research also exists on generative models that aim at capturing the (conditional) distribution(s) of brain morphology changes induced by aging and other factors (e.g., [4,10,23,33]). These generative models can then be utilized for patient-specific longitudinal predictions of disease progression, template estimation, biomarker discovery, or to systematically synthesize data to train other models. Systematic data generation or an analysis of the influence that different assumed generative factors (e.g., age, sex, or lifestyle scores) have on brain morphology variations, or the fully data-driven discovery of previously unknown factors, require a generative model to be able to effectively disentangle them in its latent space so that the user can systematically modify and control them (see [13,20] for overviews).

More recently, hybrid generative-inferential brain aging models have been proposed that explicitly tackle both tasks (brain age prediction and morphology generation) within a single, invertible model (e.g., [21,31,35]). Their key idea is to exploit the bidirectional relationship between factor estimation and factor-specific morphology generation. In [31], this is achieved by structuring the model's latent space such that the first dimension holds the age information while all remaining dimensions account for the age-unrelated identity information of the brain. During training, a supervised regression loss is utilized to map age to the first dimension, while the identity information is mapped to the remaining dimensions where it is further disentangled via factorization with a Gaussian prior. Technically, [31] uses a normalizing flow [16] to represent the invertible mapping between brain morphology and the structured latent space.

Normalizing flows (NFs) have several advantages (e.g., true invertibility and exact log-likelihood-based training) over competitive generative models [16], but they come at the cost of requiring the model's latent space to have the same dimensionality as the input space. This is a severe problem in neuroimaging where image data is often composed of millions of voxels and a major reason why existing NF models often only operate on 2D slices (e.g., [23,27]). In [31], this problem is circumvented by combining three intertwined components that allow to analyze and generate brain morphology at full resolution in 3D: 1) Brains are represented via velocity fields that encode morphological differences with respect to a template, which removes the need to represent gray value information. 2) The manifold of permissible velocity fields is approximated with a low-dimensional affine subspace of maximum data variation (= 1000 dimensions) to reduce the complexity of the problem. 3) The NF only maps the low-dimensional affine subspace representation to a similarly sized, structured latent space.

This invertible brain aging model is extensively evaluated in [31] on data from more than 5000 subjects and within several application scenarios (e.g., age estimation, template generation, patient-specific aging simulation). In this work, we utilize [31] as a starting point and extend the invertible model and its evaluation in three directions: 1) We add sex as an additional, supervised factor to the structured latent space and evaluate this combined brain aging and sex classification model on real data instead of on (partially) synthetic data as in [31].

2) We specifically evaluate the information disentanglement in the structured latent space of this combined model. 3) We propose to learn an order of the identity components of the model's latent space that sorts them according to the amount of morphological variation covered to improve efficient exploration.

2   Methods

We will first briefly summarize the NF-based invertible brain aging model (referred to as iBAM from here on) from [31] in Sect. 2.1. Then, the addition of sex as a supervised factor will be described in Sect. 2.2, before we introduce a nested dropout variant to order the model's identity-specific latent space dimensions in Sect. 2.3.

2.1   Invertible Brain Aging Model – iBAM

iBAM [31][1] heavily relies on the principles of deformation-based morphometry [2]. Instead of using structural MR images as inputs to the model, they are first registered to a brain template via diffeomorphic, non-linear image registration. For a structural MR image I, this results in a non-linear, diffeomorphic transformation $\varphi = \exp(\mathbf{v})$ that encodes the brain morphology differences between I and the template $\bar{I}$. φ is parameterized by a vectorized stationary velocity field $\mathbf{v} \in \mathcal{V} \subset \mathbb{R}^{3n_{\text{vox}}}$ with $\exp(\cdot)$ being the group exponential map from the Log-Euclidean framework and n_{vox} denoting the number of image voxels of $\bar{I}$.

iBAM then defines a learnable, invertible, and composed transformation $m = g \circ f : \mathcal{S} \to \mathcal{V}$ that maps elements from a low-dimensional structured latent space $\mathcal{S} \subset \mathbb{R}^{n_{\text{dim}}}$ (here: $n_{\text{dim}} = 1000$) to the space of velocity fields $\mathcal{V}$ and vice versa. Function $f : \mathcal{S} \to \mathcal{A}$ is a bijection and implemented as a NF using affine coupling layers [16]. It maps elements of $\mathcal{S}$ to a low-dimensional affine subspace of $\mathcal{V}$ with coordinate space $\mathcal{A} \subset \mathbb{R}^{n_{\text{dim}}}$. Because of the difference in dimensionality of $\mathcal{A}$ and $\mathcal{V}$ ($3n_{\text{vox}} \gg n_{\text{dim}}$), function g is only truly invertible for velocity fields that are elements of the affine subspace and pseudo-invertible anywhere else. Technically, $\mathcal{A}$ is defined in [31] as the subspace of maximum data variation and estimated by performing a principal components analysis (PCA) on the training data. The matrix of orthogonal basis vectors of $\mathcal{A}$ resulting from the PCA are then used as a projection operator to define g (see [31] for details).

Latent space $\mathcal{S}$ is structured in a way that its leading dimension holds the brain's (biological) scalar age value while all the remaining $n_{\text{dim}} - 1$ dimensions represent the identity information unrelated to age. Hence, $\mathbf{s} = m^{-1}(\mathbf{v})$ can be used to estimate the brain age of I by using the zeroth component $\mathbf{s}[0]$ of $\mathbf{s}$ (from here on we use a Numpy-like notation when accessing specific components of vectors.). Conversely, specifying (or sampling) $\mathbf{s}$ allows one to generate velocity fields $\mathbf{v}$ with the model via $\mathbf{v} = m(\mathbf{s})$, which can then be utilized to warp the template $\bar{I}$ to visualize the associated brain morphology. For example, fixing

---

[1] We refer the reader to [31] for a full description of all details of this approach.

age component s[0] for a given subject/velocity field and changing the identity part s[1 :] enables the generation of artificial, similarly aged brains, while fixing s[1 :] and changing s[0] allows the model's use for subject-specific brain aging simulation (see [31] for more example applications).

Training iBAM relies on the availability of a population of n_{pop} samples $\{(\mathbf{v}_i, a_i)\}_{i=1}^{n_{\mathrm{pop}}}$ of different, healthy subjects (cross-sectional data). Here, $\mathbf{v}_i$ denotes a subject's velocity field estimated by registering the structural brain scan I_i to template $\overline{I}$ and a_i is the subject's known chronological age[2]. Learning $m = g \circ f$ is then a two-step process: 1) The affine subspace portion/function $g(\cdot)$ is estimated via PCA in an unsupervised way without using age values a_i. 2) The NF part $f(\cdot)$ with parameters θ is subsequently optimized by keeping $g(\cdot)$ fixed based on a semi-supervised loss function (explanation of all parts follows Eq. (2)):

$$\mathcal{L}_{\mathrm{age}}(\theta) = \frac{1}{n_{\mathrm{pop}}} \sum_{i=1}^{n_{\mathrm{pop}}} \left(\frac{1}{2} \Big(\underbrace{\sigma_{\mathrm{age}}^{-2} \| m^{-1}(\mathbf{v}_i; \theta)[0] - a_i \|_2^2}_{\text{age regression}} \right. \tag{1}$$

$$\left. + \underbrace{\| m^{-1}(\mathbf{v}_i; \theta)[1 :] \|_2^2}_{\text{identity mapping}} \Big) - \log|\det(\mathbf{J})| \right) .$$

Minimizing this loss results in a model of the probability distribution of brain morphology conditioned on age, parameterized by $m(\cdot)$ through the change of variables formula and optimized via log-likelihood maximization (see [1,31,34]):

$$p(\mathbf{v}|a) = \underbrace{p\Big(m^{-1}(\mathbf{v}; \theta)[0] \big| a \Big)}_{\text{age}} \underbrace{p\Big(m^{-1}(\mathbf{v}; \theta)[1 :] \Big)}_{\text{identity}} |\det(\mathbf{J})| \tag{2}$$

$$\text{with } \mathbf{J} = \left(\frac{\partial m^{-1}(\mathbf{v}; \theta)}{\partial \mathbf{v}} \right) .$$

Here, $\mathbf{J}$ is the Jacobian of function $m(\cdot)$, which has a simple structure because of the chosen NF-based setup [16,31]. Furthermore, $p(\mathbf{v}|a)$ is factorized into an age-related part and an identity part. Assuming a univariate Gaussian prior with user-specified uncertainty σ_{age} for the age part, leads to the supervised L2-based age regression loss component in Eq. (1), which ensures that the zeroth dimension of the latent space captures the age information. Then, assuming a multivariate Gaussian prior with an identity covariance matrix for the identity part in Eq. (2) results in the unsupervised identity mapping part of the loss.

In summary, minimizing Eq. (1) during training 1) encourages separation of age and age-unrelated identity information in iBAM's structured latent space via supervised factorization, 2) encourages disentanglement of the identity components of the latent space via unsupervised factorization, and 3) turns iBAM into a probabilistic generative model where new data can be sampled by using the priors.

---

[2] As usual in the brain age estimation literature, we assume that for healthy subjects no difference between chronological and biological brain age exists.

2.2 Adding Sex as Another Supervised Factor

While the setup described in Sect. 2.1, encourages disentanglement of the identity components of iBAM's latent space, it cannot be assumed that any of those components directly correspond to additional semantic factors of morphological brain variations the user wants to explicitly control or analyze. However, if supervised information/labels are available for those factors for the training data, then iBAM can be modified to also explicitly map them to distinct components of its structured latent space by adding an additional regression/classification target. This is especially straightforward to achieve if they are assumed to be independent of other factors.

A specific example of such a factor in healthy brain aging is sex. To integrate sex as an additional factor into iBAM, we generally follow the proof-of-concept setup briefly outlined in [31] and first assume that the binary sex information $s_i \in \{0, 1\}$ is available for each of the n_{pop} training subjects. The goal is then to force $m^{-1}(\mathbf{v})$ to map the sex information of $\mathbf{v}$ to the first latent space component $\mathbf{s}[1]$ in addition to mapping age to $\mathbf{s}[0]$. To avoid challenges when jointly modelling a categorial factor (= sex) in addition to continuous factors of variation (e.g., age and the identity part), we interpret the sex information as a continuous variable over $\approx [0, 1]$ (see also [32]). This converts the supervised sex classification problem into a regression problem and (again) assuming a univariate Gaussian prior with standard deviation σ_{sex} leads to the updated loss

$$\mathcal{L}_{\text{age+sex}}(\theta) = \frac{1}{n_{\text{pop}}} \sum_{i=1}^{n_{\text{pop}}} \Big(\frac{1}{2} \Big(\underbrace{\sigma_{\text{age}}^{-2} \| m^{-1}(\mathbf{v}_i; \theta)[0] - a_i \|_2^2}_{\text{age regression}} \tag{3}$$

$$+ \underbrace{\sigma_{\text{sex}}^{-2} \| m^{-1}(\mathbf{v}_i; \theta)[1] - s_i \|_2^2}_{\text{sex classification/regression}} + \underbrace{\| m^{-1}(\mathbf{v}_i; \theta)[2:] \|_2^2}_{\text{identity mapping}} \Big) - \log|\det(\mathbf{J})| \Big) .$$

We choose this Gaussian prior mainly for the ease of use/integration into the existing framework. Other choices directly operating on $[0, 1]$ (e.g., a beta distribution) are theoretically preferable but require to restrict $m^{-1}(\mathbf{v}_i; \theta)$ [1] to this interval via, for example, a logistic sigmoid bijector, which was numerically less stable in our experiments than the chosen setup.

2.3 Ordering iBAM's Identity Latent Space Dimensions

Training the model based on Eq. (3) will result in a structured latent space that disentangles age- and sex-related information covered by the first two dimensions and age- and sex-unrelated identity information captured by the remaining dimensions. While the identity dimensions will be mutually independent due to the prior, they are not ordered in any way and most likely also carry a similar amount of information required to reconstruct the mapped input. This is in stark contrast to, for example, traditional PCA-based generative models where the latent space dimensions are ordered with respect to the amount of variability in the input space they cover. Such a (potentially) meaningful order of the latent space dimensions is useful when interpreting and analyzing a generative model or when manipulating input data mapped to the latent space [6]. While some evidence exists that NF-based models can implicitly learn such an order when a complex multi-scale architecture is employed [15], we want to make this order explicit and controllable in this work without architecture modifications.

Our approach follows the nested dropout idea originally introduced by [25] and first applied to NF models in [5]. The goal is to order the dimensions of the identity part of iBAM's latent space similar to PCA-based models (first few dimensions explain most of the training data variation). Nested dropout achieves this by encouraging the model to store more information in the first components by measuring and optimizing the reconstruction error of the data in the input space when only those components are utilized. A detailed mathematical derivation can be found in [5,25].

Given the mapping of a training data sample $\mathbf{v}_i$ with age a_i and sex s_i to the latent space via $\mathbf{s}_i = m^{-1}(\mathbf{v}_i; \theta)$, let $\mathbf{s}_i[k+1:] := 0$ be a version of the latent representation where all dimensions above index $k \in \mathbb{N}_{\geq 2}$ have been set to 0. Then, $\|m(\mathbf{s}_i[k+1:] := 0; \theta) - \mathbf{v}_i\|_2^2$ quantifies the L2-based reconstruction error when only using the first k dimensions of the latent space. Integrating this term into Eq. (3) with a slight relaxation of the notation leads to

$$\mathcal{L}_{\text{age+sex}}^{\text{nested}}(\theta) = \mathcal{L}_{\text{age+sex}}(\theta) + \frac{1}{n_{\text{pop}}} \sum_{i=1}^{n_{\text{pop}}} \lambda \|m(\mathbf{s}_i[k+1:] := 0; \theta) - \mathbf{v}_i\|_2^2 . \quad (4)$$

Here, λ is used to balance the traditional loss and the reconstruction error. Choosing a fixed k will now force the model to put more information into the first k latent space dimensions. However, those components will still lack an order. We, therefore, follow [5,25] and randomly sample k during training from a rapidly decaying geometric distribution $p(k) = (1-q)^{k-1}q$ where q is a Bernoulli parameter chosen by the user. Due to the random change of k during training, with smaller k values more likely than larger ones, an order of the latent space dimensions is established.

3   Experiments and Results

In our evaluation, we focus on three main aspects: 1) Brain age estimation and sex classification performance comparison when training iBAM with the three different losses discussed above. 2) Quantitative assessment of the successful disentanglement of supervised factors and identity information in iBAM's latent space. 3) Specific analysis of differences in iBAM's latent space when trained with and without nested dropout.

Data: We generally follow the experimental setup (e.g., data pre-processing) outlined in [31] and also use the same data set of T1-weighted brain MR images for our evaluation. In total, images of 5287 different healthy adults curated from five different sources (SHIP study [29], IXI database[3], SALD [30], DLBS[4], and OASIS-3 [18]; age range: 19–90 yrs; females: 55%; see [31] for details) are available for this evaluation. This data set is randomly split into training, test, and validation sets of 4281, 684, and 332 subjects, respectively, while stratifying for data source, age, and sex. The pre-processing pipeline proposed in [31] then consists of four major steps: 1) Bias field correction [28], 2) skull-stripping [14], 3) affine registration [3] to the SRI24 brain template [26] to remove major size differences, and 4) non-linear, diffeomorphic registration [12] to the SRI24 template to capture remaining morphological differences. The resulting and vectorized velocity fields with $\approx$ 17 million components serve as input data to train/use the models.

Experiments: Based on the training data, we train four different iBAM variants using the different loss functions described in Sect. 2: 1) age-only model using $\mathcal{L}_{age}$ (iBAM$_{age}$), 2) age-only model with nested dropout using $\mathcal{L}_{age}$ in Eq. (4) (iBAM$_{age}^{nested}$), 3) combined age and sex model using $\mathcal{L}_{age+sex}$ (iBAM$_{age+sex}$), 4) combined age and sex model with nested dropout using $\mathcal{L}_{age+sex}^{nested}$ (iBAM$_{age+sex}^{nested}$). All models use the same, best-performing NF architecture from [31] and are implemented in TensorFlow 2.2 using components from the TensorFlow Probability library [11]: 16 affine coupling layers to define $f(\cdot)$ where the affine scaling/translation functions are fully-connected neural networks with 2 hidden layers of width 32. The models are trained with full batches for 10k epochs using AdamW. Loss parameters were selected empirically based on [31] and the validation data and set to $\sigma_{age} = 0.14$, $\sigma_{sex} = 0.01$, $\lambda = 1.0$, and $q = 0.05$.

Table 1. Age estimation error (MAE in years), sex classification accuracy (in percentage of correctly classified subjects), as well as SAP and MIG scores for age and sex achieved by all four models on the test data. MAEs are averaged over all test subjects.

Model/Metric	Age (MAE)	Sex (Accuracy %)	SAP Age	SAP Sex	MIG Age	MIG Sex
iBAM$_{age}$	4.39 ± 3.23	n/a	0.84	0.00	0.24	0.03
iBAM$_{age}^{nested}$	4.32 ± 3.19	n/a	0.83	0.02	0.26	0.00
iBAM$_{age+sex}$	4.32 ± 3.12	93.27	0.85	0.75	0.26	0.69
iBAM$_{age+sex}^{nested}$	4.37 ± 3.25	92.84	0.82	0.71	0.25	0.61

All models are then used to estimate the test subjects' brain age and sex (if applicable). Brain age estimation accuracy is quantitatively assessed by calculating the mean absolute error (MAE) between chronological and estimated age values. Similarly, sex classification accuracy is measured by comparing the real sex values and the predicted ones when using a threshold of 0.5 on the latent space dimension. We also compute Separated Attribute Predictability (SAP) [17] and Mutual Information Gap (MIG) [7] scores with age and sex as ground-truth

---

[3] https://brain-development.org/ixi-dataset/.
[4] http://fcon_1000.projects.nitrc.org/indi/retro/dlbs.html.

factors as an additional way to assess the degree of (partial) disentanglement of iBAM's latent space depending on the chosen loss. Both scores give results in $[0,1]$ where values closer to 1.0 indicate better disentanglement. Moreover, we generate age- and sex-conditioned brain morphology templates for $\text{iBAM}_{\text{age+sex}}^{\text{nested}}$ by sampling its latent space and utilizing its generative direction as outlined in [31]. This helps 1) to verify that the model captures the typical trend of brain aging and 2) and to analyze how the model differentiates females/males.

Results: The results are summarized in Table 1 and Figs. 1, 2 and 3. Quantitative age and sex estimation results (age: MAE of ≈ 4.3 years; sex: accuracy of $\approx 93\%$) reported in Table 1 for the iBAM configurations without nested dropout are comparable to the results achieved in [31]. However, it is important to note that in contrast to [31], the combined age and sex estimation model in this work is trained and tested on real subjects instead of artificially altered data. This confirms iBAM's ability to handle multiple supervised factors in a real world setup. Adding the nested dropout component to the loss function during training, has nearly no influence on the age and sex estimation accuracy when comparing nested and standard models.

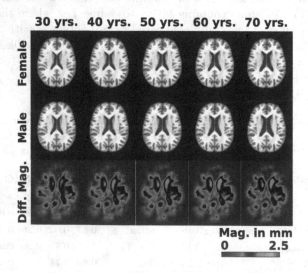

Fig. 1. The first two rows visualize age- (columns) and sex-conditioned (rows) morphology templates generated using $\text{iBAM}_{\text{age+sex}}^{\text{nested}}$. They represent the typical, sex-specific brain aging patterns covered by the model and were computed as described in [31]. The last row shows color-coded magnitude images of the non-linear transformations required to transform the female brain into a male brain at each age. They, therefore, highlight the differences between female/male brains at each age.

The age- and sex-conditioned templates generated by $\text{iBAM}_{\text{age+sex}}^{\text{nested}}$ in Fig. 1 illustrate that the combined model captures the typical trend of brain aging (e.g., growth of lateral ventricles with age). Moreover, Fig. 1 also shows that the model differentiates male and female brains (at least partially) based on ventricle size. According to the model, males have larger ventricles than females

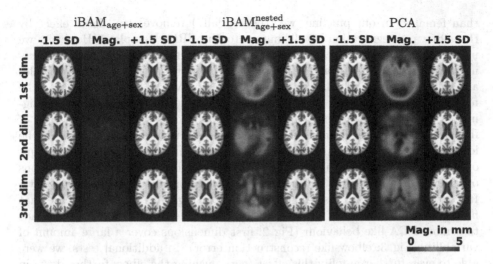

Fig. 2. Samples generated by sampling the first three dimensions (rows) of the identity latent space part of $iBAM_{age+sex}$ and $iBAM_{age+sex}^{nested}$ at ± 1.5 standard deviations (SD) for a fixed age and sex (50 years, female). For comparison, a visualization of the variation along the first three most important components of the affine subspace used as an input to the NF part is also provided (PCA), which still contains the age and sex information that is not present anymore in iBAM's identity latent space. Color-coded magnitude images (Mag.) of the non-linear transformations between ± 1.5 SD are shown for a better visual interpretation of the information covered along each dimension.

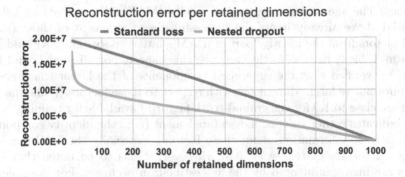

Fig. 3. Comparison of the mean reconstruction errors for all training samples (squared error wrt. affine subspace representation – averaged across all samples) when different numbers of the leading dimensions of iBAM's identity component are retained. Results are reported for $iBAM_{age+sex}$ (standard loss) and $iBAM_{age+sex}^{nested}$ (nested dropout). Unused latent space dimensions are set to zero.

at the same age (see magnitude images in Fig. 1). This effect is already visible at the age of 30 years, but the magnitude images (last row of Fig. 1) suggest that it is amplified with age. Biologically, males usually have larger brains than females. In our pipeline, we (theoretically) remove this global effect by the affine pre-registration of all images to the SRI24 template. However, we measured the ventricular volumes in those affinely registered images using segmentations propagated from the template and found that the ventricles of males are still on average 14% larger than those of females. This confirms that the model represents an effect that is present in the data after pre-processing. Figures 1, 2 and 3 illustrate the effect nested dropout has on the identity part of iBAM's latent space. From Fig. 2, it can be seen that each dimension of the identity part of the standard model's latent space only captures a small amount of variability. This effect is also visible in Fig. 3 where all identity dimensions of $iBAM_{age+sex}$ appear to be (nearly) equally important to represent the data. In contrast, $iBAM_{age+sex}^{nested}$'s results visualized in Figs. 1, 2 and 3 showcase that nested dropout establishes an order of the leading identity dimensions that leads to a more PCA-like behaviour (Fig. 2: first dimensions cover a large amount of variability; Fig. 3: elbow-like reconstruction error). In additional tests, we were able to even further amplify this effect (e.g., pushing the elbow further down in Fig. 3) by increasing the λ parameter. However, this led to a pronounced drop in age and sex estimation accuracy. Furthermore, using nested dropout helps the user to efficiently explore iBAM's identity component by focusing on the leading components. When directly comparing the first dimension of $iBAM_{age+sex}^{nested}$'s identity space and the first dimension of the affine subpace (PCA in Fig. 2), which serves as an input to the model's NF part, it can be seen that they share similarities. The differences are probably related to the removal/disentanglement of age and sex effects from the identity dimension that are still present in the affine subspace. The age and sex estimation results (MAE and accuracy in Table 1) discussed above already imply the successful disentanglement of those (supervised) factors from the identity part of iBAM's latent space. The SAP and MIG scores in Table 1, help to further analyze this aspect. For all models and both scores, we verified that the supervised components of the latent space are the most informative latent dimensions with respect to those factors. While the SAP scores are close to 1.0 for the ground-truth factor(s) available for training, which again indicates rather successful disentanglement (e.g., the identity components hold nearly no information about those factors), especially the MIG scores for the age factor are quite low (< 0.3). However, it has to be noted that those results are highly influenced by the age estimation accuracy. For example, the MIG score between $iBAM_{age}$'s estimated age values and a latent space component artificially set to a constant value for all test subjects is 0.27. We, therefore, believe that the SAP and MIG results at least show that no single component of the identity space exists that holds relevant information about the supervised factor(s). In addition, the scores achieved for sex when training age-only models (nearly zero SAP/MIG scores for $iBAM_{age}$ and $iBAM_{age}^{nested}$) also show that despite factorization, neither the standard nor the nested model's identity space features a dimension that mainly represents sex information. This is also true for the dimensions of the affine subspace for which scores of (SAP: 0.19; MIG: 0.03) for age and (SAP: 0.02; MIG: 0.01) for sex are achieved. Those results again signify the challenge of disentangling and isolating specific semantic factors of variation in a fully unsupervised way via factorization.

4 Conclusion

In this paper, we extend the invertible brain aging model from [31] and specifically evaluate its ability to disentangle age and sex from unrelated identity information. We show that adding sex as an additional supervised factor during model training results in a combined and generative brain age regression and sex classification model where age and sex are successfully assigned to single dimensions of the model's latent space. This enables the user to specifically control those factors when generating data. By adopting a nested dropout approach, we also show that the model can be trained to produce a latent space where the leading components of the identity part are ordered and cover a large amount of morphological variability. While this helps to more efficiently explore and summarize the inter-subject variability, it remains to be explored whether those ordered dimensions are helpful to identify additional semantic factors of morphological variation. Our disentanglement analysis results at least suggest that training a supervised age-only model using nested dropout does not map sex information to a single dimension of the identity part of the latent space. This is similar to the behaviour of a PCA-computed affine subspace of maximum data variation and mainly indicates that other/stronger priors are needed to achieve such a disentanglement in an unsupervised way.

Acknowledgements. This work was supported by the River Fund at Calgary Foundation. Image data used in this work were provided in part by the OASIS-3 project (Principal Investigators: T. Benzinger, D. Marcus, J. Morris; NIH P50 AG00561, P30 NS09857781, P01 AG026276, P01 AG003991, R01 AG043434, UL1 TR000448, R01 EB009352).

References

1. Ardizzone, L., Kruse, J., Rother, C., Köthe, U.: Analyzing inverse problems with invertible neural networks. In: ICLR (2019)
2. Ashburner, J., Hutton, C., Frackowiak, R., Johnsrude, I., Price, C., Friston, K.: Identifying global anatomical differences: deformation-based morphometry. Hum. Brain Mapp. **6**(5–6), 348–357 (1998)
3. Avants, B.B., et al.: The optimal template effect in hippocampus studies of diseased populations. Neuroimage **49**(3), 2457–2466 (2010)
4. Bass, C., da Silva, M., Sudre, C., Tudosiu, P.D., Smith, S., Robinson, E.: ICAM: interpretable classification via disentangled representations and feature attribution mapping. Adv. Neural. Inf. Process. Syst. **33**, 7697–7709 (2020)
5. Bekasov, A., Murray, I.: Ordering dimensions with nested dropout normalizing flows. arXiv:2006.08777 (2020)
6. Bengio, Y., Courville, A., Vincent, P.: Representation learning: a review and new perspectives. IEEE Trans. Pattern Anal. Mach. Intell. **35**(8), 1798–1828 (2013)

7. Chen, R.T., Li, X., Grosse, R.B., Duvenaud, D.K.: Isolating sources of disentanglement in variational autoencoders. In: Advances in Neural Information Processing Systems, vol. 31 (2018)
8. Cole, J.H., Leech, R., Sharp, D.J., Initiative, A.D.N.: Prediction of brain age suggests accelerated atrophy after traumatic brain injury. Ann. Neurol. **77**(4), 571–581 (2015)
9. Cole, J.H., Marioni, R.E., Harris, S.E., Deary, I.J.: Brain age and other bodily 'ages': implications for neuropsychiatry. Mol. Psychiatry **24**, 266–281 (2019)
10. Dalca, A., Rakic, M., Guttag, J., Sabuncu, M.: Learning conditional deformable templates with convolutional networks. In: NeurIPS, pp. 806–818 (2019)
11. Dillon, J.V., et al.: Tensorflow distributions. arXiv:1711.10604 (2017)
12. Ehrhardt, J., Schmidt-Richberg, A., Werner, R., Handels, H.: Variational registration - a flexible open-source ITK toolbox for nonrigid image registration. In: Bildverarbeitung für die Medizin 2015, pp. 209–214 (2015)
13. Fragemann, J., Ardizzone, L., Egger, J., Kleesiek, J.: Review of disentanglement approaches for medical applications-towards solving the gordian knot of generative models in healthcare. arXiv preprint arXiv:2203.11132 (2022)
14. Isensee, F., et al.: Automated brain extraction of multisequence MRI using artificial neural networks. Hum. Brain Mapp. **40**(17), 4952–4964 (2019)
15. Kingma, D.P., Dhariwal, P.: Glow: generative flow with invertible 1x1 convolutions. In: NeurIPS, pp. 10215–10224 (2018)
16. Kobyzev, I., Prince, S., Brubaker, M.: Normalizing flows: an introduction and review of current methods. IEEE Trans. Pattern Anal. Mach. Intell. **43**(11), 3964–3979 (2020)
17. Kumar, A., Sattigeri, P., Balakrishnan, A.: Variational inference of disentangled latent concepts from unlabeled observations. In: ICLR (2018)
18. LaMontagne, P.J., et al.: OASIS-3: longitudinal neuroimaging, clinical, and cognitive dataset for normal aging and Alzheimer disease. medRxiv (2019)
19. Levakov, G., Rosenthal, G., Shelef, I., Raviv, T.R., Avidan, G.: From a deep learning model back to the brain-identifying regional predictors and their relation to aging. Hum. Brain Mapp. **41**(12), 3235–3252 (2020)
20. Liu, X., Sanchez, P., Thermos, S., O'Neil, A., Tsaftaris, S.: Learning disentangled representations in the imaging domain. arXiv preprint arXiv:2108.12043 (2021)
21. Mouches, P., Wilms, M., Rajashekar, D., Langner, S., Forkert, N.: Unifying brain age prediction and age-conditioned template generation with a deterministic autoencoder. In: MIDL, pp. 497–506 (2021)
22. Mouches, P., Wilms, M., Rajashekar, D., Langner, S., Forkert, N.D.: Multimodal biological brain age prediction using magnetic resonance imaging and angiography with the identification of predictive regions. Hum. Brain Mapp. **43**(8), 2554–2566 (2022)
23. Pawlowski, N., Coelho de Castro, D., Glocker, B.: Deep structural causal models for tractable counterfactual inference. Adv. Neural. Inf. Process. Syst. **33**, 857–869 (2020)
24. Peng, H., Gong, W., Beckmann, C.F., Vedaldi, A., Smith, S.M.: Accurate brain age prediction with lightweight deep neural networks. Med. Image Anal. **68**, 101871 (2021)
25. Rippel, O., Gelbart, M., Adams, R.: Learning ordered representations with nested dropout. In: ICML, pp. 1746–1754 (2014)
26. Rohlfing, T., Zahr, N.M., Sullivan, E.V., Pfefferbaum, A.: The SRI24 multichannel atlas of normal adult human brain structure. Hum. Brain Mapp. **31**(5), 798–819 (2010)

27. Sankar, A., et al.: Glowin: a flow-based invertible generative framework for learning disentangled feature representations in medical images. arXiv preprint arXiv:2103.10868 (2021)
28. Tustison, N.J., et al.: N4ITK: improved N3 bias correction. IEEE Trans. Med. Imaging **29**(6), 1310–1320 (2010)
29. Völzke, H., et al.: Cohort profile: the study of health in Pomerania. Int. J. Epidemiol. **40**(2), 294–307 (2011)
30. Wei, D., et al.: Structural and functional MRI from a cross-sectional southwest university adult lifespan dataset (SALD). BioRxiv, 177279 (2017)
31. Wilms, M., et al.: Invertible modeling of bidirectional relationships in neuroimaging with normalizing flows: application to brain aging. IEEE Trans. Med. Imaging **41**(9), 2331–2347 (2022)
32. Wilms, M., Mouches, P., Bannister, J.J., Rajashekar, D., Langner, S., Forkert, N.D.: Towards self-explainable classifiers and regressors in neuroimaging with normalizing flows. In: International Workshop on Machine Learning in Clinical Neuroimaging, pp. 23–33 (2021)
33. Xia, T., Chartsias, A., Wang, C., Tsaftaris, S.A., Initiative, A.D.N., et al.: Learning to synthesise the ageing brain without longitudinal data. Med. Image Anal. **73**, 102169 (2021)
34. Xiao, Z., Yan, Q., Amit, Y.: A method to model conditional distributions with normalizing flows. arXiv:1911.02052 (2019)
35. Zhao, Q., Adeli, E., Honnorat, N., Leng, T., Pohl, K.M.: Variational AutoEncoder for regression: application to brain aging analysis. In: Shen, D., et al. (eds.) MICCAI 2019. LNCS, vol. 11765, pp. 823–831. Springer, Cham (2019). https://doi.org/10.1007/978-3-030-32245-8_91

Comparision

A Study of Representational Properties of Unsupervised Anomaly Detection in Brain MRI

Ayantika Das[1]([✉]), Arun Palla[1], Keerthi Ram[2],
and Mohanasankar Sivaprakasam[1,2]

[1] Indian Institute of Technology, Madras, India
ee19d422@smail.iitm.ac.in
[2] Healthcare Technology Innovation Centre, IIT, Madras, India

Abstract. Anomaly detection in MRI is of high clinical value in imaging and diagnosis. Unsupervised methods for anomaly detection provide interesting formulations based on reconstruction or latent embedding, offering a way to observe properties related to factorization. We study four existing modeling methods, and report our empirical observations using simple data science tools, to seek outcomes from the perspective of factorization as it would be most relevant to the task of unsupervised anomaly detection, considering the case of brain structural MRI. Our study indicates that anomaly detection algorithms that exhibit factorization related properties are well capacitated with delineatory capabilities to distinguish between normal and anomaly data. We have validated our observations in multiple anomaly and normal datasets.

1 Introduction

Brain MRI is valuable in diagnosis, monitoring, and surgical intervention planning and guidance. Numerous signs and changes are visualized in brain MRI images, which could be pathological or normal variations [6]. MRI is versatile, and various sequences are available to observe visual features of several structural anomalies, including localized discrete (e.g., tumor, hemorrhage), diffuse (e.g., inflammation), regional and global (enlargement or contraction of structures, midline shift) changes. We focus on detection of anomalies visible in the brain MRI, arising from patient related factors, explainable as geometric and photometric changes when related to normal appearance.

Normative brain atlases have been developed for quantitative neuroinformatics [17] and are used in stereotaxic neurosurgery and electrode placement, along with diagnostic decision assistance in clinical applications like stroke management. For comparative analysis, the methods assume that anomaly causes wider structural change than normal variations (we term this the compactness property of normal variations). Population averaged atlases and multiatlas methods [16] are used to cover multiple anatomical phenotypes and widen the range of applicability. These methods use intensity based registration for computing a warp or map between the brain scan and the atlas, to standardize the data, and

J. Fragemann et al. (Eds.): MAD 2022, LNCS 13823, pp. 111–125, 2023.
https://doi.org/10.1007/978-3-031-25046-0_9

study differences. The standardization can be construed as abstracting normal geometric variations through the warp and abstracting photometric variations to standardize across scanners and imaging parameters, leaving the apparent patient-related changes for comparison.

The resulting image can be ascribed to a simple additive model in 2D:

$$image = g\_normalcy(sliceno) + anomaly + inhomogeneities \qquad (1)$$

where $g\_normalcy$ is a generative process to compute a normative reference slice. We assume that anomaly effects an additive change over the generative process, co-existing in the same domain of intensities. For lesions that distort surrounding brain parenchyma (such as intra-axial lesions), the generative process includes local elastic deformation, following which the intensity variations continue to be additive. When using a population atlas such as MNI or Colin-27 [9], the generative process is trivially indexing of an atlas slice. Other data-driven methods (including ones described in the next section) built on normal data alone, can also be used for the generative process. The last component is residual uncorrelated inhomogeneities to model scanner and parameter variations left over beyond the standardization step.

Under this oversimplified model, the task of anomaly detection is reduced to one of decomposing the image domain; this however entails problems analogous to adaptive thresholding methods for detection – bias to local contrast, affecting smaller and subtle anomalies, and also subtle global changes.

In this study, continuing with the premise of unsupervised comparative methods for modeling anomaly, we analyze some selected methods, restricting them to use only normal data, and seek to elicit an understanding of their functioning from the standpoint of factorization.

2   Approaches for Modeling Anomaly

Supervised learning techniques, known to have achieved high performance in detection, localization, and delineation of pathologies in MRI [7], are specific to a few types of lesions like tumor and stroke [11], and biased by the available annotations at training time (which are laborious to obtain).

Contemporary studies [2] explore unsupervised techniques, towards building disease-agnostic models for pathology detection and delineation [3]. Being trained only with normal data, test time pathological data (out-of-distribution) are expected to result in performance degradation in the task of reconstruction, offering a means of flagging anomaly. Auto-encoders are a well-known approach used in literature, formulated as jointly learning to encode image $x \in \mathbb{R}^{m \times n}$ (m and n are the height and width of the image) into an embedding $z \in \mathbb{R}^d$, and learning to decode the embedding to reconstruct the image $\hat{x}$. Notationally, $z = f_\theta(x); \hat{x} = g_\phi(z)$, where f_θ is the encoder and g_ϕ is the decoder.

Compatible with unsupervised learning, the detection step is possible at the output (where a noticeable reconstruction error $\delta(\hat{x}, x)$ is expected for the out-of-distribution anomalous test data) or at the embedding space (where embedding of the anomalous test data z_a is expected to deviate from the normative embedding distribution $P(z_n)$).

2.1   Selected Methods

We select the following methods for modeling normal brain data:

1. **VAE** - VAE forms a baseline for the unsupervised anomaly detection setting we have considered. VAE imposes $P(z_n)$ to be multivariate Gaussian with learnable mean and variance (weak i.i.d assumption). The underlying assumption is sufficiency of a simple Gaussian latent distribution for explaining normal data. VAE is implemented by including a Kullback-Leibler (KL) divergence regularization term along with a reconstruction term $\delta : |x - \hat{x}|_1$ in the network loss function, and trained with data using routine optimization methods like stochastic gradient descent (SGD);

2. **FactorVAE** [12] - FactorVAE also imposes $P(z_n)$ to be a multivariate Gaussian. Like VAE, the KL divergence and reconstruction term are included in the loss function, but it also includes an additional Total Correlation (TC) penalty for independence between variables in z. The independence in z aids in the better encoding of meaningful normal features within the dimensions of z.

3. **SSAE** [4] - A Laplacian scale-space Auto-encoder, which declaratively performs image domain multiband factorization into high- and low-frequency content, processing the Laplacian pyramid band-wise through independent sparse convolutional Auto-encoders and forming the reconstruction image by combining the multiresolution outputs back into a Gaussian pyramid;

4. **Glow** [14] - Generative Flow, learns a bijective mapping $f_\theta : X \to Z$ from the data space into a multivariate standard Gaussian distribution. The learning process is based on the *change of variables* formulation. The reversible transformation follows due to the bijective nature, resulting from the architectural choice of layers. The selected methods are described in Appendix A.

The latent space convention for the set of methods (VAE, FactorVAE, and SSAE) which are derivatives of the Auto-encoder family, is to have embeddings ($z \in \mathbb{R}^d$) of much lower dimension as compared to the input image space. But, GLOW is architecturally bound to have an embedding space dimension equated to the total number of pixels in the image space ($d = m \times n$). The conventional usage of the low dimensional embeddings in the former set of methods is attributed to the fact that the latent space of the Auto-encoders must have limited information capacity to prevent them from learning trivial identity functions [10]. Additionally, reconstructions of VAE suffer from image quality degradation if there are high levels of increment in the latent dimensions. The latent dimensions of VAE can be increased only up to a certain range, beyond which the generation process does not benefit from the introduced variability [20]. Thus, we have carried out experimental evaluations adopting the conventional architectural formulation of the selected methods, allowing the inter-method dimensional variations in the latent space.

2.2 Hierarchy of Properties

Our chosen methods exhibit some properties closely relatable to factorization, at the latent embedding z (via f and loss terms), and the output $\hat{x}$ (via g and loss terms). The specific properties of interest in increasing order of capability for solving the task of unsupervised anomaly detection under consideration, are discussed below:

1. **Compact organization** - proximal representation of normal variations;
2. **Separable representations** - distinctiveness within groups of variables in z (or embedding subspaces) representing normalcy and anomaly, disentangling both the groups;
3. **Controllable representations** - observe controlled changes in $\hat{x}$ via perturbing z;
4. **Identifiable features** - visual features of image space captured in embedding subspaces.

As the properties are to be observed at z and $\hat{x}$, we resort to the following intuitive ways of evidencing them:

– Studying the two dimensional spectral embeddings[1]; in order to analyze linkages between the latent vectors and comment upon their proximities. The spectral embeddings are computed using a non-linear dimensionality reduction technique which deploys spectral decomposition of z.
– Performing Local Outlier Factor (LOF)[2] analysis on z to examine the separability, in order to comment upon the distinctness of representations between the normal and anomalous sets. LOF gives a Local Outlier Detection (LOD) score, which is computed by estimating the local density deviation measured in a certain neighborhood.
– Introducing variable perturbations on z to investigate changes in $\hat{x}$ and infer upon the nature and extent of controllability in both the domains.

3 Experimental Setup

We take MRI brain scans of only healthy individuals for the training phase and include both healthy and pathological scans for the testing phase. The healthy set consists of T2 weighted MRI scans from CamCAN [18], IXI [1] and HCP [19] and the anomaly set consists of T2 weighted High Grade Glioma (HGG) data from BraTS 2017 [15]. The training and testing datasets follow the regimes as mentioned below:

– Training set: We have considered a set of 100, 100, and 26 volumes from IXI, CamCAN, and HCP datasets respectively; in order to impart better modeling capability in the presence of data from multiple sources.

[1] http://surl.li/cirgr.
[2] http://surl.li/cirgo.

– Test set: We have taken four sub-categories, in order to facilitate the investigation of the factorization properties under consideration:

- *Normal*: A set of 100 volumes 50 each from IXI and CamCAN;
- *Noisy*: A simulated pathological dataset generated by adding random patches of Gaussian noise to the Normal set;
- *BraTS*: A set 100 volumes from BraTS HGG dataset;
- *Only Pathology*: Only the pathological extractions from the BraTS set, by masking out the healthy regions.

A sequence of standardization protocols are applied to minimize the variations within the images that are incurred during the acquisition process. We perform affine registration of all the images to Colin-27, which transforms the spacing of all axial slices to 0.5 mm with in plane resolution of 0.5 × 0.5 mm. We take corrective measures to remove inhomogeneties from the scans through N4 bias correction. The brain mask for the Colin-27 atlas is used to curate brain regions through the removal of skull and other unrelated anatomical regions. Also, the intensity profile of the images is matched with the Colin-27 atlas by using histogram matching.

For modeling the Auto-encoder based approaches that we have selected (VAE, FactorVAE, and SSAE), the generalised encoder-decoder architecture from [3] is adopted. Although they share the same architecture, the representational learning of latent space is defined by the training protocol, which is different amongst them. VAE captures the latent space with dimensionality value d equal to 128. The training specifications for VAE include; training of the model for 80 epochs, usage of L1 loss for supervision of the reconstruction term, and the weightage to the KL Divergence term is adjusted using β-annealing methods till 10 epochs and then made consistent throughout [8]. FactorVAE shares a similar training strategy as VAE but with an additional Total Correlation (TC) penalty term. The weightage to the TC term is linearly annealed from 0 to 0.35 for 30 epochs and then set to a constant value throughout the training process of 60 epochs. The SSAE is modeled with three Auto-encoders operating at different levels in the Laplacian pyramid and is supervised with the L1 reconstruction loss at all three levels with equal weightage to each of them. The latent space is captured with dimensionality d equal to 1024, 256, and 64 for all the three Auto-encoders respectively. The model is trained for 50 epochs.

For modeling Glow, the architecture from [14] is adopted. The training is carried out till the data is transformed into a fixed latent representation, with its dimension d equal to 16,384. The objective function is based on the *change of variables* formulation which consists of a Gaussian function and determinant of Jacobian of the model. The former term penalizes the deviation of the model's latent representation from the fixed Gaussian and the latter reflects a local change in the volume incurred by the model. Both the penalty terms are weighted equally throughout the training process of 50 epochs. All the methods use Adam optimizer with an initial learning rate of 10^{-4} [13].

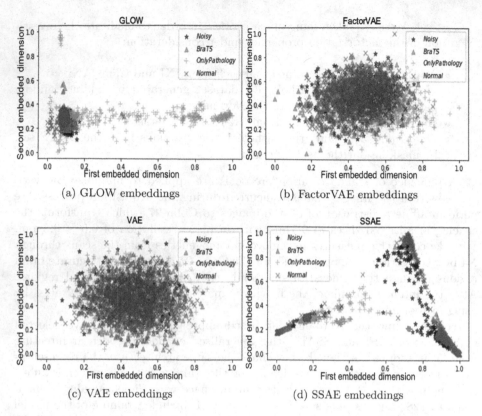

(a) GLOW embeddings   (b) FactorVAE embeddings

(c) VAE embeddings   (d) SSAE embeddings

Fig. 1. The two dimensional Spectral embeddings extracted from the high dimensional latent vectors of the Normal, BraTS, Noisy and Only Pathology test set categories as elaborated in Sect. 3 for all the four methods. The embedded space clearly depicts that the latent representations of the Normal set (in-distribution), from the (a) GLOW method, has a proximal and compact structure with distinctiveness as compared to the other out-of-distribution sets (BraTS + Only pathology + Noisy). The embedding space of the (b) FactorVAE and (c) VAE forms elliptical structures with less density. The distinctiveness property is completely missing from (c) VAE but the (b) FactorVAE has pushed away the only Pathology set to some extent. The embedding space from (d) SSAE neither adheres to any certain shape nor forms a compact structure.

4   Observations

The observations pertaining to the four properties for the different test set categories; Normal, out-of-distribution (BraTS + Noisy + Only Pathology) are described below, highlighting comparative aspects between all the four methods.

How compact and distinctive are the spectral embedding of the latent vectors?

The Fig. 1 depicts the two dimensional spectral embeddings of the latent vectors. The organization of the latent vectors in the lower dimensional spectral embedding space is leveraged to carry out the analysis.

1. *GLOW:* From Fig. 1a it is evident that the GLOW method is able to learn compact and proximal representations for the Normal set, which is surrounded by the representations of the other three out-of-distribution sets, with different degree of overlap. The degree of overlap in the Only Pathology set is very minimal with most of the samples pushed away from the Normal set in a less dense fashion. The BraTS and the Noisy set have relatively dense representations as compared to the Only Pathology set and their degree of overlap with the Normal set is high. *Thus, GLOW is seen to achieve a compact representation within the Normal set, with semantically relevant separation of the embeddings of the out-of-distribution set, disentangling meaningfully between the two sets.*

2. *VAE:* From Fig. 1c, it is seen that all the spectral embeddings of VAE are contained in an elliptical structure, which is much lower in density when compared to the GLOW embeddings. The Normal set does not uniquely hold the notion of proximal representations, rather the embeddings from all the sets are distributed in a similar manner. *Thus, VAE presents a compact representation of embeddings by entangling both Normal and out-of-distribution sets within an elliptical structure, with no separation formed between any of the sets.*

3. *FactorVAE:* Similar to the VAE, the embeddings of the FactorVAE approximates an elliptical structural formulation as in Fig. 1b. Compared to VAE, FactorVAE has relatively better proximity within the Normal set and distinctiveness between different sets; the deviation of the Only Pathology set from the concentrated region of the Normal set is visible. *Thus, the notion of compact representations in FactorVAE is similar to VAE but it highlights better properties of separability.*

4. *SSAE:* The embeddings from SSAE are neither structurally bound nor proximal for any of the sets, as shown in Fig. 1d. The samples from the Normal set have formed certain smaller groups in different regions within the embedding space. *Thus, representations from SSAE are not compact for any of the sets, with multiple separations within the Normal set, making separations amongst sets less evident.*

Which method shows delineation between Normal set and out-of-distribution set based on LOD score?

The Fig. 2 represents the histogram of the LOD scores, calculated over the frequencies of brain slices for Normal and out-of-distribution sets. The histogram plot from Fig. 2a highlights that samples from the out-of-distribution set have a long tail on the left region of the plot and the Normal set is densely populated and contained within the right half. This behaviour *showcases delineatory properties in GLOW*, despite having certain overlapping regions between the two distributions. The other histogram plots Fig. 2b, c and d does not exhibit delineatory properties in the latent space.

What is the nature of controllability in the reconstructed images ($\hat{x}$) due to different settings of perturbations in the latent vectors?

We have introduced scalar multiplicative factors (m) to perturb the latent space representations ($z*m$). The Fig. 3 highlights the dependency of the change in $\hat{x}$ due to the introduced perturbations in latent space. All the adopted methods are sensitive and show monotonic increment to the perturbations, but the degree of sensitivity is method specific. The GLOW method exhibits the highest sensitivity to the perturbations as compared to the other methods. The VAE, FactorVAE, and SSAE show much staggered changes to the perturbations. *Thus, GLOW shows highly sensitive and monotonic controllability to these perturbations as compared to other methods.*

We have experimented with another form of perturbation in the latent space, by corrupting a set of consecutive coordinates of the latent vectors, leaving all other coordinates undisturbed. The corruption is introduced in two folds Case I and Case II. For both the cases, out of all dimensions d in a latent vector, a certain set of consecutive coordinates p-q were changed and the remaining d-(p-q) were unchanged. Also for both the cases, p coordinate values are equal, but q coordinate values for Case II is greater than Case I, implying that perturbations in Case II are extended to a relatively larger span. Table 1 indicates the numerical values taken by p and q for all the methods in both the cases and the effect of these perturbations in $\hat{x}$. In both Case I and II, $\hat{x}$ from GLOW show the effect of perturbation within certain consecutive rows, while the other methods show dispersed effect throughout the spatial extent of the images. For GLOW in Case II, when the perturbations get extended to consecutive coordinates of z, the $\hat{x}$ also transmit this to an extended set of consecutive rows. These sets of descriptive qualifiers from the Table 1 are pictorially depicted in Fig. 4 for the GLOW method. The orange and blue notations signify Case I and Case II respectively. *Thus, GLOW shows localized and proportional controllability to these perturbations, while the other methods are only responsive to these changes without any specific nature.*

How does latent space perturbations affect the identifiable visual features in the image space?

From the Table 1, we can comment that SSAE, FactorVAE, and VAE disperse the effect of perturbations (within a few latent dimensions), over the entire image space (brain and background regions). But, *GLOW is highlighting the effect of perturbations within the brain boundaries*, as shown in the residual images of the Fig. 4. Although regions within the brain boundaries are affected, but not necessarily different identifiable and meaningfully relevant compartments of the brain.

5   Inferences and Discussion

The relatability of the properties under consideration to the *task of unsupervised anomaly detection* is discussed below, connecting to the observations from our methods and their reasoning.

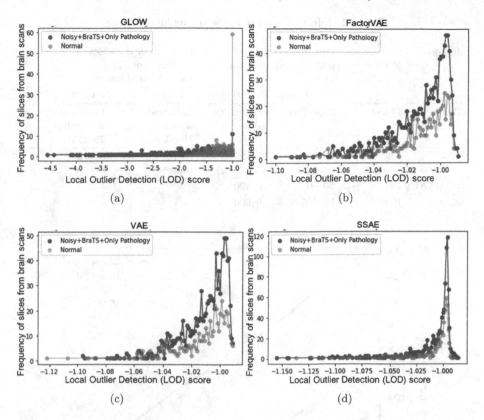

Fig. 2. The histogram plot of the Local Outlier Detection (LOD) scores with the frequency of brain slices for the Normal set and out-of-distribution set (BraTS + Only pathology + Noisy). The LOD score is evaluated on the latent space components directly. The histogram plot from (a) GLOW highlights that the out-of-distribution set has a very heavy tail on the left hand side and the Normal set is mostly centered on the right side, showing delineatory properties. The histogram plot for (c) VAE, (b) FactorVAE, and (d) SSAE does not exhibit delineatory properties in the latent space.

Relating Compact and Separable Representations to the Task: The separation between the representations of the Normal and out-of-distribution set is quite essential for modeling anomaly detection in the unsupervised setting we have considered. This holds from the fact that our unsupervised setting assumes representations of the out-of-distribution (test) set will be separated from the representations of the Normal (training) set, which will result in performance degradation in the former set indicating anomalies. Our observations have made us conclusive of the fact that separability within the representations is a consequence of the property of compact organization within the Normal set.

– GLOW is the only method that is able to show compact organization within the Normal set and so it is able to disentangle and create separation between the sets. GLOW is able to show this property because it has learned to map

Table 1. Effect of perturbations in the latent space

Methods	Dimensions of z (d)	Perturbation defined from p to q coordinates of latent z		Location of the effect of Perturbations in reconstructed image	
		Case I (p-q)	Case II (p-q)	Case I	Case II
GLOW	16,384	6500–7000	6500–8000	Localized within Rows 75–95	Localized within Rows 75–125
VAE	128	50–90	50–120	Dispersed over the entire Image	
FactorVAE	128	50–90	50–120		
SSAE	1024	50–150	50–600		

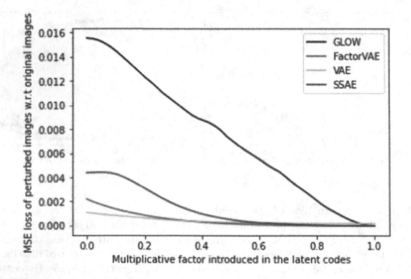

Fig. 3. The dependency of latent space perturbations with change in the reconstructed image space, captured through Mean Squared error (MSE). Perturbations are in the form of $z*m$, where z is the latent vector and m is the multiplicative factor, with values ranging from 0 to 1. Effectively, an increasing order of perturbation in the latent space arises from decreasing values of m, implying $m = 1$ has no change on z. MSE values are calculated between reconstructed images (due to varying values of m) and the original images. The GLOW has higher sensitivity to the perturbations followed by SSAE, FactorVAE, and VAE in decremental order of their sensitivity nature.

the image space to a high-dimensional standard Gaussian, whose dimensionality is equal to the image space. This has enabled it to capture attributes more meaningfully and semantically relevant to the image space.

– VAE is entangling representations for Normal and out-of-distribution sets, enclosing representations from all these sets to an elliptical structure, since it has learned to map the image space to a much lower dimensional standard

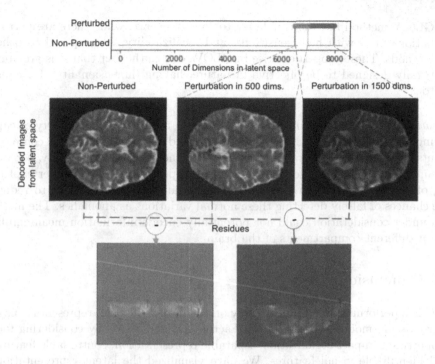

. **Fig. 4.** The top row pictorially depicts the introduced perturbations for the GLOW method with Case I and Case II, as in Table 1. The second row highlights the reconstructed images (left to right) for non-perturbed z, perturbed z for 50 and 1500 dimensions respectively. The third row shows the residue (differences after subtracting) of the reconstructed images due to perturbations w.r.t the non-perturbed image. They are reflecting localized and proportional effects.

Gaussian. VAE needs to learn the reconstruction task to make the representations meaningful, while this task constrains the assignment of higher dimensions to z. This bottleneck entangles all the representations without any separation between them.

- FactorVAE also encloses representations within an elliptical structure since it shares a common objective with VAE but it has better separability since an additional term is introduced in the objective to ensure statistical independence amongst vectors in the latent space.
- SSAE is not capable of encoding compact and separable representation, since it learns a transformation for the Laplacian of the images at different scale spaces without any constraint in the formulation to the latent space.

Relating Controllable Representations to the Task: It is essential to observe controlled changes $\hat{x}$ while there are perturbations in z, for the task of anomaly detection that we have considered. In order to indicate the separation of the latent representations for Normal and out-of-distribution sets in $\hat{x}$, it is crucial for the anomaly detection task to transmit changes in z to $\hat{x}$. The transmission of changes in $\hat{x}$ should be sensitive to the extent and location of perturbation in z to localize anomalies.

– GLOW method has the capability to control over $\hat{x}$, while there are perturbations in z, with high sensitivity and localizability as compared to other methods. These properties arise in GLOW due to the fact that it is architecturally designed to be bijective in nature, having dimensionality of z equal to $\hat{x}$.

Relating Identifiable Feature Representations to the Task: The property of capturing the dimensions of z with identifiable and visually meaningful compartments of the brain is hierarchically at the highest level of capability, for our unsupervised anomaly detection task. This property can enable better capturing of the features for variations of normal brain information so as to reduce the chances of falsely detecting these normal variations as anomalies. The methods under consideration could not potentially encode information meaningfully about different compartments of the brain.

6   Conclusion

We have performed an empirical study on the nature of latent representations of four existing models; GLOW, VAE, FactorVAE and SSAE by considering four properties; compact organization, separable representation, controllable features and identifiable visual features. We have visualized the latent representations in a reduced dimensional space, inferred on LOD score and introduced perturbations to compare the properties for the different methods. We observed that the GLOW method is able to show compact representations, with meaningful separation and controllability. We have discussed explicitly how the properties relate to the task of unsupervised anomaly detection. We are able to conclude that GLOW is a potential candidate for the unsupervised anomaly detection since it exhibits better properties of factorization, which are closely related to the end task.

A   Appendix

A.1   VAE

VAE [5] enforces the learning of marginal likelihood of the training data(x) in a generative setting. This learning process has an objective of maximizing the lower bound of the likelihood, written as:

$$\log p_\theta(x|z) \geq L_{VAE} = \sum_{i=1}^{N} [E_{q_\phi(z|x)}[\log p_\theta(x_i|z)] - D_{KL}(q(z|x_i)||p(z))] \quad (2)$$

The notations ϕ, θ denote the parameterization of the encoder and decoder in the VAE, z is the latent representation, N is the number of training samples, $D_{KL}(\|)$ is non-negative Kullback-Leibler (KL) divergence, p(z) and q_ϕ(z—x) are the prior and posterior distributions respectively.

Although, from the theoretical perspective there seems to be no bound on the prior and posterior distributions, but to make the optimization of the objective function in 2 tractable both the distributions are approximated to be Gaussians with diagonal covariance matrix. Specifically, the prior distribution is set to standard Gaussians $P(Z) = \mathcal{N}(0, I)$. The encoder in our VAE setup takes healthy brain image x as input and then estimates the mean and diagonal covariance matrix of the posterior for the given input sample. These estimated parameters are used to sample the latent vector corresponding to the input healthy scan through "reparameterization trick". The reparameterization technique is introduced to enable gradient calculation with respect to the parameters of the encoder which is generally not feasible in this scenario. The sampled latent vector is passed through the decoder to generate the reconstructed image $\hat{x}$.

A.2   FactorVAE

FactorVAE [12] closely shares modeling components and optimization objectives with VAE along with some additional constraints on the latent space. The trade-off between the two objective components in VAE does not allow the posterior to achieve factorial nature similar to the prior. This factorial nature would enhance the independence of the latent vectors and thus would add more interpretability. The objective for FactorVAE is given as:

$$L_{FactorVAE} = \sum_{i=1}^{N}[E_{q(z|x)}[\log p(x|z)] - D_{KL}(q(z|x)||p(z))] - \gamma D_{KL}(q(z)||q'(z))$$

(3)

where, q(z) = $E_{p(x)}[q(z-x)]$, $q'(z)$:=product of (q(z_j)) (j = 1: d), d is dimensionality of z. The objective 3 augments a new component called Total Correlation (TC) to the objective function of VAE, which minimizes the KL divergence between the marginal posterior q(z) and its factorial representation $q'(z)$, but these terms are generally not tractable. So, a discriminator (D) is used to estimate the density ratio that arises in the TC term. The discriminator basically classifies latent vectors coming from each class q(z)/$q'(z)$, while encouraging the vectors to be factored.

A.3   GLOW

GLOW [14] learns an invertible nonlinear transformation between input distribution and independent latent distribution. The invertibility is facilitated by the fact that the layer is designed to have bijective properties. Such bijective layers are cascaded to increase the capacity/expressiveness of the model. This non-linear, but invertible, mapping together with the change-of-variables would lead to a tractable and closed form solution of the marginal likelihood representing the healthy images as in:

$$\log p(x) = \log p(z) + \log |det(df_\theta(x)/dx)|$$

(4)

where, p(z) is the prior, f_θ is the encoder, $\det(df_\theta(x)/dx)$ determinant of Jaccobian of the model.

This likelihood is decomposed in terms of 1) a fixed latent distribution, which is a standard Gaussians $P(Z) = \mathcal{N}(0, I)$ and 2) Jacobian of the model, constituting the training process. Since, GLOW learns an invertible mapping, explicit training for the decoder is not required. The encoder itself will uniquely determine the decoder. Due to bijective mapping, each point in the input space is uniquely represented by a latent code. Similarly, distinct latent codes are mapped to non-overlapping input images.

A.4 SSAE

SSAE [4] is an Auto-encoder based methods that model normalcy without any additional constraint in the latent space forms the most widely used baselines for pathology detection in unsupervised settings. SSAE disentangles the high and low frequency of the input data by learning to compress and reconstruct the laplacian pyramid of healthy MRI brain scans. Our application requires laplacian pyramid at four levels (K = 0, 1, 2, 3). Images at each level k is denoted as:

$$I_k = d(g_\sigma(I_{k-1})) \qquad \forall \, 0 < k \leq K, \tag{5}$$

where I_0 is the input image x, g_σ ($\cdot$) is a gaussian kernel with variance σ, d($\cdot$) is a downsampling operator. The high frequency residuals H_k at each level k is denoted as:

$$H_k = I_k - u(I_{k+1}) \qquad \forall \, 0 \leq k < K \tag{6}$$

where u($\cdot$) is an upsampling operator. An image x is completely represented by the low-resolution image I_K after K downsamplings and the high frequency residuals $H_0, \dots H_{K-1}$. the final reconstructed image is obtained via the following:

$$\hat{x} = \sum_{k=0}^{K-1} [u(I_{K-k}) + H_{K-1-k}] \tag{7}$$

References

1. IXI Datatset. http://brain-development.org/ixi-dataset/
2. Atlason, H.E., Love, A., Sigurdsson, S., Gudnason, V., Ellingsen, L.M.: SegAE: unsupervised white matter lesion segmentation from brain MRIs using a CNN autoencoder. NeuroImage Clin. **24**, 102085 (2019). https://doi.org/10.1016/j.nicl.2019.102085
3. Baur, C., Denner, S., Wiestler, B., Navab, N., Albarqouni, S.: Autoencoders for unsupervised anomaly segmentation in brain MR images: a comparative study. Med. Image Anal. **69**, 101952 (2021). https://doi.org/10.1016/j.media.2020.101952
4. Baur, C., Wiestler, B., Albarqouni, S., Navab, N.: Scale-space autoencoders for unsupervised anomaly segmentation in brain MRI. In: Martel, A.L., et al. (eds.) MICCAI 2020. LNCS, vol. 12264, pp. 552–561. Springer, Cham (2020). https://doi.org/10.1007/978-3-030-59719-1_54

5. Burgess, C.P., et al.: Understanding disentangling in β - VAE. arXiv preprint arXiv:1804.03599 (2018)
6. Cenek, M., Hu, M., York, G., Dahl, S.: Survey of image processing techniques for brain pathology diagnosis: challenges and opportunities. Front. Robot. AI **5**, 120 (2018)
7. Gudigar, A., Raghavendra, U., Hegde, A., Kalyani, M., Ciaccio, E.J., Rajendra Acharya, U.: Brain pathology identification using computer aided diagnostic tool: a systematic review. Comput. Methods Programs Biomed. **187**, 105205 (2020). https://doi.org/10.1016/j.cmpb.2019.105205
8. Heer, M., Postels, J., Chen, X., Konukoglu, E., Albarqouni, S.: The OOD blind spot of unsupervised anomaly detection. In: Medical Imaging with Deep Learning, pp. 286–300. PMLR (2021)
9. Holmes, C.J., Hoge, R., Collins, L., Woods, R., Toga, A.W., Evans, A.C.: Enhancement of MR images using registration for signal averaging. J. Comput. Assist. Tomogr. **22**(2), 324–333 (1998)
10. Jing, L., Zbontar, J., et al.: Implicit rank-minimizing autoencoder. Adv. Neural. Inf. Process. Syst. **33**, 14736–14746 (2020)
11. Kaka, H., Zhang, E., Khan, N.: Artificial intelligence and deep learning in neuro-radiology: exploring the new frontier. Can. Assoc. Radiol. J. **72**(1), 35–44 (2021). https://doi.org/10.1177/0846537120954293
12. Kim, H., Mnih, A.: Disentangling by factorising. In: Proceedings of the 35th International Conference on Machine Learning, pp. 2649–2658. PMLR (2018). ISSN 2640-3498
13. Kingma, D.P., Ba, J.: Adam: a method for stochastic optimization. arXiv preprint arXiv:1412.6980 (2014)
14. Kingma, D.P., Dhariwal, P.: Glow: generative flow with invertible 1x1 convolutions. In: Bengio, S., Wallach, H., Larochelle, H., Grauman, K., Cesa-Bianchi, N., Garnett, R. (eds.) Advances in Neural Information Processing Systems, vol. 31. Curran Associates, Inc. (2018)
15. Menze, B.H., et al.: The multimodal brain tumor image segmentation benchmark (brats). IEEE Trans. Med. Imaging **34**(10), 1993–2024 (2014)
16. Mori, S., Oishi, K., Faria, A.V., Miller, M.I.: Atlas-based neuroinformatics via MRI: harnessing information from past clinical cases and quantitative image analysis for patient care. Annu. Rev. Biomed. Eng. **15**, 71–92 (2013). https://doi.org/10.1146/annurev-bioeng-071812-152335
17. Nowinski, W.L.: Evolution of human brain atlases in terms of content, applications, functionality, and availability. Neuroinformatics **19**(1), 1–22 (2020). https://doi.org/10.1007/s12021-020-09481-9
18. Taylor, J.R., et al.: The Cambridge centre for ageing and neuroscience (Cam-CAN) data repository: structural and functional MRI, MEG, and cognitive data from a cross-sectional adult lifespan sample. Neuroimage **144**, 262–269 (2017)
19. Van Essen, D.C., et al.: The human connectome project: a data acquisition perspective. Neuroimage **62**(4), 2222–2231 (2012)
20. Yeung, S., Kannan, A., Dauphin, Y., Fei-Fei, L.: Tackling over-pruning in variational autoencoders. arXiv preprint arXiv:1706.03643 (2017)

Author Index

Printed in the United States
by Baker & Taylor Publisher Services

Printed in the United States
by Baker & Taylor Publisher Services